MY BEST FRIEND

RALPH

MY BEST FRIEND RALPH

Michael Prestigiacomo

ISBN 979-8-218-06399-3 (paperback)
ISBN 979-8-218-06400-6 (ebook)

Published by Ruff Ruffington LLC

Library of Congress Control Number: 2022916394
First Printing: 2022
Printed in the United States of America

Cover photos by Renee Ostrowski
Text photos by Renee Ostrowski and Michael Prestigiacomo
Family photo on page ix by John Ohnstad

For Ralph and Renee

CONTENTS

Introduction 1

Ch. 1 -- Cats are for girls 7

Ch. 2 -- Dogs of war 19

Ch. 3 -- Cat tales 29

Ch. 4 -- Cat named Peter 37

Ch. 5 -- Return policy 47

Ch. 6 -- Barriers and beans 57

Ch. 7 -- Ding dong . . . visitors 69

Ch. 8 -- Who needs sleep? 79

Ch. 9 -- Mouse in the house 91

Ch. 10 -- The Trojan cat 105

Ch. 11 -- First floor mayhem 119

Ch. 12 -- Let's go camping 133

Ch. 13 -- What's for dinner? 149

Ch. 14 -- Who's watching Ralph? 161

Ch. 15 -- The Mild Kingdom 173

Ch. 16 -- Lost and found 185

Ch. 17 -- Aloha 197

Ch. 18 -- Love of *Nature* 209

Ch. 19 -- The purr-fect patient 221

Ch. 20 -- New Year's Day 235

Ch. 21 -- Another year 247

Epilogue 255

Acknowledgments 263

Memories 265

INTRODUCTION

One evening after midnight in the fall of 2011, I was having trouble getting to sleep. I eventually rolled over in the dark toward my wife, Renee, and attempted to plant a kiss on her cheek, only to encounter a face-full of fluffy cat hair and a single lick on my nose from a wet, rough tongue. I had already forgotten about our new "roommate" who preferred to share Renee's pillow with her every night. As I rolled back to my spot, I knew that my life, as I once knew it, would never again be the same.

Less than a week later, I heard a "ker-plunk, splash." While Ralph was trying to sneak into the bathroom to munch on plants, he had jumped straight into the toilet, not realizing "someone" forgot to put the toilet lid down. Clinging to the rim with his front paws, he was startled and confused as we lifted him out of the toilet bowl.

I joked to Renee that I should have flushed the toilet and given him a whirlpool bath. She did not laugh, nor did she approve of my suggestion to use her hair dryer to dry off his soaking-wet, long hair. After she dried him with my bath towel, I was left to mop up the floor while promising to always make certain that the toilet lid was closed. I doubt that Ralph was the only cat to ever take a dive into a toilet but, regardless, I made a conscious effort so that it would never happen again.

A month later—"splash"—he slipped and fell into the basement laundry tub next to the washing machine as it was going through the rinse cycle. I happened to be nearby, watching him frantically leap out of the tub and onto the top of the washing machine. Knowing so little about cats, there was only one thing I could do. I started yelling, "Reneeeeee... get some towels... 'your' cat got wet again... and he's covered with suds." And that was just the first of several issues that day.

At 62 years of age, I had spent most of my working life solving problems and dealing with difficult situations, and now I was looking forward to the benefits of a leisurely retirement. Renee and I renewed our passports, purchased new suitcases, and were ready to go. But nothing in my past prepared me for what I thought was so simple as adopting a cat, leading to the biggest, most monumental challenge of my entire life. Perhaps even more surprising, I never liked cats, I never owned a cat, and I never wanted a cat.

This was all Renee's fault. She is a life-long cat lover and shelter volunteer. She adores cats and persisted with these subtle suggestions that "we" needed one. I eventually agreed, with the caveat that "I" got to pick it out, despite knowing nothing about cats.

At first glance, Ralph captivated me with his thick orange hair and bright round eyes. He was so docile, but appearances can be deceiving. The moment his paws touched the floors of our house, things immediately spiraled out of control. There was nothing fuzzy or cute when Ralph routinely cleared everything off my desk, destroyed my tax returns, and nearly made a multimillion-dollar stock market trade on my laptop. And late at night, he frequently turned off my CPAP machine, used to counter my sleep apnea.

He wasted no time knocking out our internet wireless connection, disabling our stereo system, tampering with my laser and photo printers, yanking out the cables from behind our TV, unplugging the DVD player, and disconnecting all three land-line phones. Most dangerous and horrifying of all was when he started biting and chewing on all our lamp cords, electrical cables, and the wires on our charging stations.

He also tripped me up multiple times while I was coming down the stairs, once nearly launching me through the second-floor window, which would have been fatal. Equally concerning was his disregard for danger, including his fascination for sitting on the kitchen counter next to the gas stovetop or standing nearby as baking pans came out of a very hot oven. On occasion he even ventured into our dishwasher while we were loading or unloading dishes.

As a first-time, late-in-life cat owner, I was struggling with these major disruptions and adjustments to my lifestyle, made even more difficult by the added responsibility for Ralph's safety and healthcare, the latter of which I found to be unexpectedly expensive. I can get my car serviced for less.

During his first visit to a nearby, small-animal clinic, I was surprised to hear that Ralph needed a course of antibiotics for a previously undiagnosed illness, one he got before arriving at the shelter. But getting a pill down his throat was nearly im-possible. Pill pockets did not work; he knew they were a trick. It would have been easier to feed the pill to a mouse and then release the mouse in our dining room for Ralph to catch and eat. Such a novel idea for giving him his medication.

How could I be so foolish? I was told that owning a cat was supposed to be full of comfort and joy, but apparently someone mixed up that metaphor with Christmas, because Ralph and Rudolf had nothing at all in common.

As I contemplated writing this book, I was astounded to read that there are more than 95 million domestic cats resid-ing throughout all 50 states, plus millions more around the globe—a few of which I have personally seen in such places as rural Japan, the ancient ruins of Rome, and in the vast urban areas of Istanbul. Feral, stray, and pet cats are a common sight just about anywhere in the world, and wherever we traveled, Renee always made certain that I took notice.

I was also amazed to read that one out of every three households in America has at least one cat, the average being two. That led me to ask, "Why would anyone want to read a book about 'my' cat?" My rationale was simple. I am a person who has disliked cats for my entire life, and then along came this three-year-old orange cat with an unknown background who languished in a shelter for three months while waiting to be adopted.

Looking back at his first 48 hours in our house, I was ab-solutely certain that rescuing him was the most bone-headed, life-altering mistake that I had ever made, so much so that I ac-tually inquired twice about returning him. While I frantically sought advice from other cat owners, a sad-looking Renee sat in our living room clutching her furry new friend and fearing that at any moment he would be taken from her arms and surrendered back to the shelter.

Admittedly, I knew nothing about owning, caring, or understanding cats; that was Renee's specialty. And yet in a moment of weakness and against my better judgment, I relented. Ralph got to stay.

Meanwhile, whatever limits or boundaries I set for Ralph, he repeatedly ignored. The more he aggravated me, the greater *his* satisfaction and enjoyment. Perhaps my biggest mistake was believing that I could tame an untamable cat who had a distinct advantage. He had not yet revealed his high degree of socialization, intelligence, and cunning.

As I recount my erratic life with Ralph, I suspect you will be familiar with the dilemmas I faced, perhaps even nodding your head in agreement, while often criticizing my many missteps and recognizing my utter ignorance. Amid such chaos and turmoil, I also believe you will find my journey with Ralph to be poignant and heartwarming.

I never imagined that a simple stray cat could open my mind and heart to such a degree that he would one day become my friend.

ONE

Cats are for girls

ARCHAEOLOGICAL EVIDENCE REVEALS that more than 4,000 years ago the ancient Egyptians revered cats, even worshiping them as deities and intermediaries to their gods. Laws protected them from being killed and often upon their death, they were mummified and buried in special gravesites. Orange happened to be a popular color for cats, often depicted on surviving murals. Further proof from unwrapped cat mummies actually revealed remnants of orange fur.

Researchers have also credited the Egyptians for their early efforts at large-scale domestication and care for their cherished felines. Other cultures in the region were not as enamored, appreciating cats mainly for their rat-catching abilities in the holds of their ships.

Eventually, merchants throughout the Mediterranean region introduced cats to the Romans who appreciated them not just as pets, but for protecting their farm fields and stores of grain from vermin. There is also evidence the Vikings had developed an affinity for cats, both as pest controllers and companions. Even their goddess, Freyja, had a chariot drawn across the sky by two cats. Although there is no factual evidence, many believe that orange was their preferred cat color, perhaps because there are so many ginger cats in that region today.

Meanwhile, as the Vikings spread across the continent so did the proliferation of cats. But in the 15th century, various religious groups in Europe began to view cats negatively, linking them to the devil and to satanic rituals, in spite of their benefits to seafarers and farmers. In that era, black cats were even demonized in various religious myths and superstitions.

Quite frankly, I never believed that nonsense about black cats, but I did side with the Egyptians and Vikings on one thing—I did like the color of orange cats, as long as they weren't mine to keep or care for.

One evening in the fall of 2011, Renee and I were deeply engrossed in our favorite PBS drama, when I was forced to hit the pause button as another type of drama began to unfold on the couch next to us. Our new cat, Ralph, that we just adopted several weeks earlier, was beginning to wake up from a nap. After going through his "stand and stretch" maneuver, he eased himself down onto the carpet, passed under my legs, and was now perched atop my desk, just a few feet away.

I was not worried. I already knew his plan, and this time I was prepared. Ignoring him, I hit the "play" button on the

DVD player, allowing the characters on TV to resume their discussion. And just as I had expected, Ralph proceeded directly across my desk and sat on my new laptop, not realizing that a day earlier I had designed and built a sturdy wooden cover, three inches high, to protect it.

He looked confused, even tossing a "meow" to get my attention, perhaps thinking I had not seen him. But I had. As I turned away from him and toward Renee, I started laughing as I remarked, "Now he can sit there all night, for as long as he wants." With my laptop safe and secure, I returned to the climax of our TV show, while Ralph turned his attention to my HP laser printer, an ancient monster of a machine that still functioned very well and had recently been "cat proofed."

Four rolls of toilet paper stacked on top of the protruding paper tray created a barrier to prevent him from standing on it, so I thought. His weight would certainly snap off that delicate piece, with no possibility of me finding a replacement tray for such an old and reliable copier.

Ralph then began pushing those toilet paper rolls off the top of the tray, one roll at a time, looking back at me to see if he finally had my attention. I still ignored him. Once all the rolls were on the floor, Ralph stepped delicately on top of the paper tray in triumph. The tray should have immediately snapped off, sending both cat and tray plunging to the floor below. Nothing happened, and I laughed again.

Throughout my career, my specialty had been "anticipation." I never doubted Ralph's persistence, so I had previously placed two paperback books under the tray for support. It held; I won. But he was not giving up. Even with the volume on the TV turned up, I could hear pens, markers, framed photos, and assorted knickknacks all being "pawed" off my desk. Then he slapped my desk phone out of its charging station and began digging under the six one-pound bags of dry beans—my version of sand bags—that covered and protected all the phone and electronic wires on my desk.

Ralph and I made brief eye contact, a sort of stare-down, while I remained seated and continued to ignore him. He turned again, deciding to make a perilous climb to the top of that enormous laser printer, a difficult ascent considering that six rolls of paper towels and an empty sealed box blanketed the summit. Once atop the unstable peak, he made a striking pose as though he were the reincarnation of Edmund Hillary, conqueror of Mt. Everest. There were no meows and no noise of any kind. He only wanted my attention. I simply covered my head with his tiny baby blanket, the material being so thin that I could see through it, which allowed me to continue to watch TV.

Ralph was not pleased. He quickly skidded down from his mountain, causing an avalanche of paper towels and toilet paper. After jumping off the desk, he ran to the couch and peered under his blanket to confirm I was really there. Then came the pawing and the meowing. I gave up, tossing his blanket aside and wondering just what it was that he wanted. The answer was the same as what any seasoned cat owner would expect—nothing, other than to get my attention. And then for no apparent reason, he jumped off the couch, left the room, and headed for his bowl of kibble.

Every evening the same routine: first napping next to us while we watched TV, then getting up and going to my desk to incite trouble, but to what end?

Meanwhile, the rolls of toilet paper that he kept knocking off the paper tray started coming unwound, so I put painter's tape around each of them, and then taped all four rolls to the printer. It was funny watching Ralph trying to paw them off the tray. They would not budge. But he wiped that silly smirk off my face when he starting using both paws to undo them, so I simply added more tape. He then upped his game, adding more cat-power.

I surrendered. Besides, every time I wanted to load more copy paper into the tray, it was such a hassle to peel away all the tape. Perhaps because I gave up, he did, too. But the truce did not last long. He soon focused on a new target, leaping onto our six-foot-long entertainment cabinet and positioning himself directly in front the television to block our view. I tried to ignore him, but having a cat in the foreground of every TV show was very distracting.

After realizing that he was too small to block much of the 50-inch screen, Ralph opted for a new strategy, carefully walking behind the TV to do some electrical "maintenance" such as unplugging the wires and chewing on them. About every 30 seconds, he would pause his "work" and peek out from behind the back of the television to see if he had my attention yet. I pretended I was not concerned, until the TV screen went black.

Renee rushed into the room, trying to coax him out from one side, while suggesting that I let go of the remote control and lend some help. With great dexterity, she reached behind and gently lifted him out, then carried him to the living room couch where they sat together in sweetness and harmony. But not for long. Ralph soon jumped down, ran though the dining room and around the corner to the TV room, now frustrated because I had closed the door.

I was busy trimming and fitting two empty Kleenex boxes to cover and protect all the wires and cables. For added security, I taped them to the base of the cabinet and to the back of the TV with heavy-duty packing tape. The result looked like a flat-screen TV with a hideous growth on its back.

While I had been cat-proofing the TV, Ralph remained in the hallway pounding on the door and meowing loudly. "Can't you hear him crying for you?" Renee called out to me. "He sounds so sad... he just wants to come in and see you."

I knew better. Ralph was a modern-day Trojan horse, or more appropriately, a Trojan cat. If he gained entrance, he would resort to mayhem and destruction.

Once I was satisfied that all the electronics were properly protected, we had our "grand opening." Renee brought in popcorn and refreshments, and I turned on the TV, while Ralph settled back in his spot on the couch and napped. Life was back to normal... for a while.

A week or so later, Ralph raised the bar to an extreme and dangerous level when he went behind the TV again. This time, he stood on top of those newly installed Kleenex boxes and stretched to the top of the television, where we could just see his soft paws poking over the top, sending chills down my spine. I was horrified to imagine that he might tip the large, flat-panel television off the cabinet and send it crashing to the floor. The thought of a possible electrical fire bursting out in the room and burning down the house scared me silly.

I called the store where we made our purchase, asking to buy a simple, short bracket to secure the top of the television to the wall, ensuring it could not tip over. The salesperson said no such thing existed. There were only brackets for wall-mounting the whole television, which we did not want to do. When I explained I wanted some type of safety bracket to prevent our cat from knocking over the TV, there was a bit of silence. Then he transferred me to another department. No one ever answered. I continued to search the Internet. There were no cat-protective TV brackets. Evidently, no one else ever worried about their big-screen TVs being tipped over by their cats.

After voicing my concerns about Ralph potentially knocking over the TV and starting a fire, Renee became very concerned, but not for the reason I expected. She was only worried about Ralph, not our house. For his safety, she insisted that I replace all our fire alarms with new ones and buy a radon detector for good measure. Then I was tasked to examine our fire extinguisher in the basement to ensure it was still operable.

All this talk of fire prevention prompted a new, mutually agreed upon safety rule. Ralph could never be left in the TV room "unsupervised." When it was time for bed, Renee would scoop him from the couch and close the door behind her as she carried him upstairs to our bedroom.

In hindsight, how could I ever have foreseen that owning a cat would be fraught with so many problems and distractions? Even the simple act of watching TV was much more difficult, thanks to Ralph stepping on the remote and messing up the settings. Twice in one month I had to call the cable company and ask them to talk me through resetting it.

Renee was never bothered by Ralph's mayhem. She took it all in stride. Ralph was "her boy," and she would stand by him regardless. All of his behaviors that I thought were terrible, Renee viewed as cute and humorous. When I wanted to squirt Ralph with the water bottle, she wanted to envelop him with hugs and kisses. Her calm demeanor and life-long experience with cats afforded her a positive perspective. She also reminded me that Ralph was a cat, not a wild horse that needed to be tamed.

For all that to resonate with me, I needed time—actually much more time—and plenty of patience. And yet for some unknown reason, Ralph enjoyed messing with my mind, my desk, and the television. And his bad behaviors in the TV room were minor compared to the dozens of his transgressions throughout the rest of the house.

It is important to remember that for most of my life, I always disliked cats and never wanted one. Perhaps Ralph picked up on that. So how did I evolve from loathing him to loving him? The easiest way to understand such enlightenment is to take the proverbial ball of yarn and unroll it all the way back to my childhood, following this lengthy journey leading to the present.

Back In 1953, at the ages of two and four, my little brother John and I moved with our parents into a new house in Monona Village, a suburb on the outskirts of Madison, Wisconsin. The highlight of our young lives was when my father brought home a large wooden box called a "television," capable of receiving three TV channels. A year later, they added another station, an *adults-only* channel called WHA/TV, something to do with public broadcasting.

The advent of television opened a whole new world of adventure for John and me, including an introduction to what we now wanted most—a dog.

We were enthralled by shows like Rin Tin Tin, which featured a wonderful German Shepherd living on a military outpost in the 1880s with a young orphan boy named Rusty. Later came "Sergeant Preston of the Yukon" and his Alaskan Husky, Yukon King. Other shows with dogs followed: Roy Roger's dog, Bullet, and Sky King's dog, Shadow.

I had no idea of various breeds. My only requirement for our new dog was that it had to be "big." John and I begged our parents for years for a dog, but Dad worked a full-time job and painted houses on the side. With a growing family and a tight budget, there was no room for Rin Tin Tin's brother to join our household. And then one day, Dad came home after visiting Mom in the hospital. He had a big announcement. No, we were not getting a dog; instead, we would be getting another sister.

As for our neighborhood, I knew of only one family that had a dog, a Collie mix, that bonded only with its family and barked at everyone else. I also never recalled seeing anyone in our neighborhood "walking a dog." It was the same for "jogging." In that era, neither had yet to become a popular part of our culture. At the same time, I knew of no family that had a cat, or admitted to it. I just assumed cats were solitary, unsociable pets that probably slept a lot and ranked in the same category as pet turtles and parakeets.

Typical of the times, I associated cats with girls and dogs with boys. But I do recall a time in grade school when a girl in our class was telling the others that her parents wanted to get her a kitten, which prompted an insensitive boy to say that he was going to get a boa constrictor that would eat her cat. That remark made her cry. I actually felt sad for the girl and never forgot that conversation because I always hated snakes and was smart enough to know that a boa would eat the boy first before trying to swallow the girl's little cat. Aside from that episode, I found cats to be mostly fictional, except for the feral ones that I saw at my cousin's farm. Those were wild and unfriendly.

Meanwhile, I soon lost all hope for a dog; yet past desires have an unusual way of reviving themselves. During the seventh grade, my parents "encouraged" me to get a newspaper route, earning me a whopping six dollars a week. I was living "large" and doing quite well, until the unexpected hit me with a vengeance—winter in Wisconsin!

I never saw it coming; snow and paper routes do not mix well. My new red bike with an embarrassingly large basket mounted on the front was useless for delivering newspapers on snow-filled streets. Adding to my misery, the Sunday morning edition was about two inches thick and quite heavy. I dreaded those mornings. Mom or Dad would wake me up at 5:30 a.m., while brother John got to stay in bed. Even more disheartening were the below-zero temperatures with new fallen snow drifting to my knees.

My dad's solution for helping me was to attach a wooden box to my sled so I could haul more newspapers and maybe finish my route before midnight, so it seemed.

As I trudged through the snow, I contemplated polar explorers trekking across the South Pole, similar to my forging new pathways up all those snow-covered driveways. No matter how I tried, there was nothing glamorous about it. Admiral Byrd required a plane to get to the South Pole, while my needs were much simpler. To successfully complete my Sunday morning expeditions, I needed to a buy a pair of skis and somehow attach them to the metal runners of my sled. Then I had to convince Dad that "we" needed a large Alaskan Husky. It continued to be a very long winter.

Following grade-school graduation, I made a big decision to leave home and go to the seminary. I wanted to become a priest. God had called, not just for me, but to one-third of the boys in my eighth-grade class. As for my brother John—who never helped me out on those frigid Sunday mornings—he was forced to inherit my paper route. However, he eventually got the last laugh. Our parents finally got a dog, and John was allowed to give up that paper route.

After four years of high school and two years of college in the seminary, I relinquished my vocation and transferred as a junior to the University of Wisconsin in Madison. Those were turbulent times. The Vietnam War was raging in Southeast Asia, sparking widespread student protests and creating a huge distraction on campus. After three semesters, my interest in education evaporated. I needed to take a break.

In the spring of 1971, I enlisted in the Army in a special program, volunteering for a one-year tour of duty in Vietnam in a combat position of their choice—infantry, armor, or artillery—with a guarantee of a six-month early release on my two-year commitment. During the previous eight years, I had developed a fascination with Southeast Asia, devouring dozens of books and countless news magazines on current events and past histories of that region of the world. I was now getting my wish to travel to Vietnam to witness history first-hand, except that I would be going as a soldier, not as a tourist.

Any thoughts of ever getting my own dog were now a distant memory; and as for cats, I still disliked them.

TWO

Dogs of war

EVERY TEN YEARS, the U.S. government conducts a national census. While all households and occupants are counted, their pets are not. That task is done by private sector groups that gather and share their valued information with the pet food and pet supply industries, as well as with the veterinarian community to gauge the need for their products and services. These pet population tallies are difficult to compile, but estimates indicate that half of all households in the U.S. have at least one dog, and more than 40% of all households have at least one cat, the average being two.

During my childhood, our family fell in the "zero pets" category, despite my brother and I hopefully begging for a dog. Instead, our parents opted for more children. I could not have imagined that at 22 years of age, my chances of having a pet would be realized when two things intersected in my life—the army and dogs.

In December of 1971, I was aboard a military cargo plane destined for the sprawling Army and Air Force base in Bien Hoa, just north of Saigon. The plane landed at night and as it taxied to the terminal in the midst of a monsoon rain, an incoming rocket exploded nearby. The flight engineer yelled out to us, "Welcome to Vietnam."

The Army had chosen to put me through artillery training, after which I volunteered to become a paratrooper, solely for the challenge and thrill of parachuting out of planes. But after arriving at the replacement depot in Bien Hoa, I waited for days to hear which remote artillery base I would be assigned to, and then fate struck.

"Can any of you write?" asked an officer who wandered among us. I wasted no time in raising my hand.

"Yes, sir," I replied. "I wrote for my school paper and have more than three years of college." After glancing at my file, the lieutenant gave me a nod and told me to report to the PIO—the Public Information Office. At that moment, I became an "Official U.S. Army Correspondent" with the 3rd Brigade of the 1st Cavalry Division—no horses, only helicopters. My new job was to venture out on assignments, write stories, and assist with the brigade's monthly newspaper, *The Garry Owen*.

The PIO was a small group of about a dozen people. We enlisted men were the writers, editors, graphic artists, and photographers. The officers handled public relations, which included interacting with U.S. and foreign journalists.

The first person I met in our unit was Bill Waite, a photographer and fellow Wisconsinite. He took me under his wing and found me an empty bunk in his "hooch," slang for our living quarters that were built of 2x4s, screening, and corrugated metal roofs. Row upon row of these hooches loosely resembled the set of the TV series *M*A*S*H* and, admittedly, our lifestyle had some similarities. Before I was able to unpack, Bill introduced me to their mascot "Zero," a medium-sized, orange and white dog, best described as a mixed breed, with long hair, a curled tail, and a great disposition. Most importantly, this friendly and lovable mutt really liked me. And after all these years, I finally got a dog, even if I had to share him with eight other guys.

Throughout the following weeks, while we were at work or on assignment, Zero roamed freely all day with a motley group of a dozen other dogs of all sizes. Large, medium, and runts. The base was like a giant dog park with every other hooch having its own mascot. However, I never recall seeing any dog food, so our pets typically ate what we ate. This meant that their favorite hangout was by the door of the mess hall where a sign read "Do not feed the dogs." Below the notice someone had scrawled "Because it will kill them." Actually, the food was pretty good, so packs of dogs showed up with military precision when it was time for breakfast, lunch, and dinner.

Several months into my tour, our buddy Zero became quite ill and, sadly, he had to be put to sleep. Shortly thereafter, Bill ended his tour, and the new replacements were not interested in finding another dog. My interest had also faded, until one morning near the end of May. After an uneventful night on guard duty, I was taking a shortcut back to our hooch when a guy I had never seen before came around the corner.

"Hey," he said with a smile, "Do you want a dog?" Half asleep and still in a daze, I could barely see what he was holding, and then he added, "She was the runt of the litter, and she needs a new home."

Before I could respond, he handed me a three-pound puppy. I had no idea what to do. Should I look in her mouth or examine her paws? I had always wanted my own dog, but it was supposed to be "a very big dog." Much too tired to think clearly, I just nodded to him and said "OK..."

As he walked away, I yelled "thanks," although I wasn't quite sure why until I lifted this tiny thing up to my face for a proper "hello." She was a mixed breed, as most were, with a short gray coat and a curly tail, and so full of enthusiasm. She was also incredibly cute.

After cradling her in one arm like a football and using the sleeve of my other arm to wipe wet kisses off my face, I said, "Come on, Daisy, let's go see your new home." That was the first name that popped into my head. As I walked along, she kept looking up at me so excitedly. This made me smile, until I realized how little I knew about caring for such a young dog.

There was no "puppy chow," so on my trips to the mess hall I requested additional strips of bacon or extra servings of meat, and trimmed them into bite-sized pieces for her. For such a small dog, Daisy had a great appetite, which was remarkable, considering that other guys were also bringing back leftovers for her. A borrowed cereal bowl from the mess hall made a perfect water bowl, but there were no "pooper scoopers," probably because no one really cared.

During Daisy's first week, I started taking her to the office in the mornings. With carefree enthusiasm, she loved trotting

My puppy Daisy in Bien Hoa, Vietnam, after she had an
accident under a sergeant's desk.

alongside me, taking eight steps for every one of mine and leaving tiny paw-prints on each side of a furrow plowed in the sandy soil by her little, rotund belly. She was obviously well fed. Because of her otherwise diminutive size, I often carried her in the hip pocket of my olive-drab fatigue pants. She fit perfectly, with just her head and front paws poking out like an Australian joey in its mother's pouch. We seldom went far before being waved down by guys who wanted to pet and admire her.

At our office, Daisy would park herself on the floor next to my desk and nap. Unfortunately, she also started peeing under the staff sergeant's chair. I decided it was best to leave her back at the hooch where she was relatively safe and could run around all day with a posse of canine pals. At the end of the day, I often found her napping outside the door of our hooch, stretched out and lying in a shallow hole that she dug in the sand to cool herself from the heat and humidity. When she saw me approaching, she would get so excited, jumping up and running to meet me.

For her sleeping arrangements, I folded three towels in a circle on the floor directly under my cot. She loved it there, and I soon realized that this little dog could be just as wonderful as any big dog I'd wanted as a kid.

As for my job at the PIO, I was not the most prolific writer in our unit, but I did learn a great deal about journalism and photography. By the summer of 1972, after I had just completed several of my best stories, my buddy Dave from the administration section flagged me down with the news, "We're going home!" All tours were being cut short; transfer orders were in process. I was being reassigned to the PIO office in Ft. Riley, Kansas.

It was a bittersweet moment. I was going back to the States, but Daisy would have to stay behind. In fact, all dogs had to remain, including the hundreds of military scout and guard dogs who were designated as "excess baggage." To my relief, many friends who were not leaving quite so soon begged me to give them Daisy. One particular fellow pleaded with such sincerity that my only response was, "Take good care of her," and he promised.

On our last day together, Daisy sat next to me on the ground outside our hooch while I petted her head and rubbed her belly. When several other dogs came running past, I gave her an extra-long hug and said "goodbye" as she rushed off to play with them. She was a popular dog and had made so many new friends, both canine and human. She was also unaware that I was leaving. In hindsight, Daisy and I had such memorable fun despite being together for only six weeks. Decades later, as I reflected on my time in Vietnam, I realized I had never seen any cats there. Perhaps I was not looking closely. Besides, how could any cat be as cute, loving, and personable as my Daisy?

After my discharge from the Army in the fall of 1972, I returned to the University of Wisconsin and completed my degree in Economics, courtesy of the G.I. Bill. With the country weathering another recession, I returned to my old part-time job in the bindery at Webcrafters, a large printing company. Three years later, I decided to become a full-time employee with actual benefits.

In 1977, I bought my first house, a duplex or two-unit as some call them in the Midwest. I resided on the ground floor, while renting out the upstairs space. Shortly after my first tenant moved in, she acquired a pair of Siamese cats. While introducing them to me as they lounged on the second-floor stairway, one of them made a lightning-fast swipe across my cheek and drew blood. That really hurt, and it did nothing to endear me to felines.

A few months later, she purchased a colorful parakeet and hung its cage from the ceiling of her living room. The next evening, she arrived home in time to see the bird being swallowed whole. Evidently, one or both of her cats had made an incredible leap straight up to the underside of the cage, clinging to it while managing to open the door. That bird had no chance against those wily cats.

Meanwhile, after I'd spent several more years working in the bindery, the company took advantage of my education and abilities, and moved me to customer service. That change allowed me to purchase a nicer house located only blocks from work. However, the house needed to be completely gutted and remodeled. Only the brick exterior and the maple floors would survive.

Built in 1920, this one-and-a-half story house had no insulation, substandard wiring, an antiquated bathroom, and a room that I guessed was a kitchen, but with no counter space. The original mechanicals in the basement—the boiler, plumbing, and electrical panel—all needed to be replaced. Considering my passion for the PBS series *This Old House*, I was thrilled to take on this two-year home remodeling project, which turned out to last nearly ten years. With the majority of my free time allotted to remodeling, and the house an on-going worksite, it was impossible to have a pet.

Around the same time, I was surprised to learn that some

of my friends actually owned cats. I called them "ghost cats." The only signs of their existence were the food and water bowls on the kitchen floors, with never a cat in sight. The owners explained that their cats often preferred to hide under beds when guests arrived and would only come out when the strangers were gone. I was not impressed.

As for my five sisters, only one ever adopted a cat, but "Rascal" was solely for her young boys, and not for her. I still recall one night when I stayed at her house, sleeping in the guest bed. Unfortunately, the summer humidity was extreme, and her house had no air conditioning. Even with an open window, the dense, hot air was downright oppressive, but that wasn't the only reason I didn't sleep well.

I was awakened several times by the sound of "crunch, crunch, crunch." Rascal, the cat I had never seen, was somewhere in that dark bedroom snacking from his one-gallon gravity-fed kibble station. Also, during the night, my sweat-soaked body felt like it had been coated with bread crumbs. Between the itchiness and the humidity, it was impossible to sleep. I felt miserable. The following morning my sister explained that Rascal often slept in that bed and was known to track litter onto the sheets. That's when I realized that my arms and legs had been coated in cat litter, providing a whole new meaning to the expression "shake-and-bake."

My other encounters with cats are equally memorable. After agreeing to meet at the home of an acquaintance, I vividly recall walking through the front door and immediately reaching out to pet his large plump male cat. It was relaxing in a cloth chair that was quite torn and ragged. This should have been my first clue. As I stroked his head a few times, I noticed that everyone in the room had stopped talking. They just stood looking at me in disbelief.

"Did you just pet that cat?" they asked in unison.

"Yeah... he's nice," I said as I reached out to pet his head again, and what a surprise! That twenty-pound tomcat let out a "growl," not a hiss, and took a swipe at my hand with his large lion-like claws. I pulled my arm back so fast that if anyone had been directly behind me, my elbow would have knocked them unconscious. Everyone in the room laughed, while its owner seemed satisfied that his overweight cat was still acting as it should—mean and ornery.

As we all headed out the door, I noticed a wet spot on the back of my hand. It was blood. I never felt the contact, but it sure started to hurt. Ten minutes later, the incident was forgotten. However, it did cement my general dislike for cats.

THREE

Cat tales

HOW MANY LIVES do cats really have? The answer tends to vary among the myths and cultures throughout time. During the Middle Ages, some residents of southwestern Europe believed that cats had seven lives, while regions in the Middle East held to six lives. Then there is the centuries-old English proverb, "All cats have nine lives."

Even William Shakespeare, who was no fan of cats, used the phrase "nine lives" when he described a villainous character in *Romeo and Juliet*. Such references about cats surely stem from their physiological makeup that allows for their flexibility, balance, and quickness. They are indeed stealthy, cunning survivors. However, one fact is crystal clear—all cats only have one life.

SEVERAL BLOCKS FROM our house, Renee witnessed a cat jumping from a second-floor balcony onto a cement sidewalk in pursuit of a rabbit. The cat survived; the rabbit did not. Compare that incident to our friend's cat who simply rolled out of bed in the middle of the night and severely tore a rotator cuff in its back leg, causing permanent injury.

On other occasions, I have heard sensational news reports about cats that fell from high-rise buildings and survived. Those are nice stories, except that for every cat who lived to meow after such a fall, most make a premature journey across the Rainbow Bridge. This "nine lives" belief is bogus, while a more realistic saying from a popular old metaphor, "Curiosity killed the cat," is not so far-fetched.

WHEN IT COMES to near tragedies with cats, my brother John is a good example of someone who exercised great care and concern for his two adopted domestic short-haired kittens: a male named Corky, and a female, Scooter. But it is John's retelling of early incidents that sends chills up my spine.

Early one morning about 40 years ago, John was on his way to work and paused to say "goodbye" to his kittens, except that Scooter was nowhere to be found. After searching all the rooms in his house, he hurried down to the basement recreation room as a last resort, but still no Scooter. John was now perplexed and late for work, but heading back up the stairs, he thought he heard a muffled "meow" coming from the other side of the wall—but she was not in the next room.

Then he heard another sad, barely imperceptible "meow" and was struck with the heart-pounding realization that Scooter was actually *inside* the wall.

That little kitten had managed to climb up a tall bookcase and squeeze through a suspended ceiling tile. After walking around up there in total darkness, she had tumbled down between the interior wall studs and was trapped. And there was no escape. Without hesitation, John used his bare fist to punch several holes in the drywall, then carefully reached inside to pull out Scooter. If John had not been so concerned and vigilant, Scooter may not have survived.

Not long after Scooter's incident, Corky swallowed a pine cone from the Christmas tree, which led to a very expensive surgery. John would have sacrificed his own needs in order to provide proper care for his cats, and he was also well aware that cats had only "one life."

For most of my life, I was never aware that my brother loved cats so much. Considering all the times I visited his house, I never saw them, and it's not surprising since they were a common indoor breed called "scaredy-cats."

Aside from my puppy Daisy in Vietnam, my life remained "pet free" and my desire for another dog had long since faded. I was now focused on my new sales job that necessitated a move to Boston in 1996. With a long-term plan to return someday, I decided not to sell my house in Madison and chose to rent a one-bedroom apartment in a 26-story high-rise building in the middle of Boston's Back Bay. I expected this small apartment to be a temporary arrangement, but I remained there for 14 years, selling textbook printing to major publishers.

Adapting to my new life in this historic city was easier than I expected. Within three blocks of my apartment there were several banks, a post office, the Boston Public Library, the Amtrak station, several subway stops, two shopping malls, a grocery store, and twenty restaurants. The Boston Public Garden and Boston Common were only a ten-minute stroll away. Also, my professional career progressed better than I imagined, and within four years, my personal life would change forever after a chance encounter with a woman who would one day become my wife.

One morning in 2000, I walked from my apartment to Houghton Mifflin, a major publisher, to discuss a new college textbook that our company would be printing for them. While reviewing specifications for this title with Marie, a manufacturing buyer, I caught a glimpse of a woman walking past her cubicle. I leaned back so far in the visitor's chair that I nearly tumbled into the hallway.

"Hey, Marie, who was that woman that just walked by?"

"Oh, that's Renee. She's the new administrative assistant, and she is so nice."

As I raised my eyebrows and flashed a Cheshire grin, Marie slapped me on the knee and laughed. "Oh yeah... I know what you're thinking."

After my meeting with Marie, I meandered around the 6th floor of the college division searching for Renee's cubicle, and returned the next day to introduce myself. In the weeks that followed, I often took detours to her area, always stopping to chat for a few minutes. Over the course of our discussions, I discovered that Renee shared a flat with roommates in Cambridge and took the bus home to New Hampshire on weekends. I also learned that we had a mutual connection on three topics: gardening, international travel, and the Boston Red Sox. However, there was a fourth interest of hers, her favorite of all, for which she exuded much enthusiasm. Her love of cats. It was much easier for me to focus on the first three topics, while merely pretending that I was interested in all her cat stories.

Renee has treasured cats her whole life. Her first was Becky, an overweight tabby. After it had passed away, her family adopted a kitten named Arthur, a long-haired, orange tabby with white coloring. Renee said they were inseparable. He followed her everywhere throughout the house and slept in her bed every night until she left home for college.

As I became better acquainted with Renee, I invited her to a Red Sox game, where we chatted for all nine innings in the farthest row of the upper deck. After declining my offer of a "Fenway Frank" hotdog, I discovered that she is a lifelong vegetarian. "Strike two." Her first strike was her obsessive love of cats.

Continuing with baseball parlance, she never struck out during our first season together. We made good teammates, and I was pleased that I did not strike out either, nor did she decide to trade me. We continued to spend more time together, building on our friendship as we frequently walked among our favorite spots: the Public Garden, the Boston Common, the Freedom Trail, Quincy Market, and the North End. And with our shared appreciation of history, we enjoyed all of Boston's landmarks and museums. However, during our long conversations, there was one topic that Renee kept repeating so often—her love of cats.

My knowledge of cats bordered on pure ignorance. I believed that cats were just little critters without much character. However, when I realized how serious Renee was with this cat business, I forced myself to pay closer attention, or at least to pretend. But then Renee had to complicate matters, explaining that various cats could easily be identified by the color of their coats—calico, tortoiseshell, tabby, dilute tabby, tabby-calico, bi-color, bi-color tabby.

I wrote down a page of notes, but accidentally misplaced them. I later realized that I would never be able to remember all these details. I found it easier to categorize cats as "short hair, long hair, black, brown, multi-colored, and 'unusual.'" That was much simpler, until Renee explained that there were more than 60 different species of cats, all descended a million years ago from the original species called *Felis silvestris*.

One aspect of her explanation made perfect sense. I now understood why the most popular cat names are "Felix" and "Sylvester." But retaining all this other information was nearly impossible. I much preferred to focus on where we were going to dinner on the coming weekend.

Over those early years together, Renee continued to reminisce about her many fond memories of cats, or "cat tails" as I called them. One of her favorite stories took place during her childhood in New Jersey. Her friend Kelly's cat, Cindy, would always wait for them at the bus stop after school. The three of them would then walk to Kelly's house and play together. I found that story touching, but also extremely hard to believe. Cindy's behavior sounded more like a dog than a cat.

Obviously, cats were Renee's favorite creatures, and she had loved Becky and Arthur very much. But what concerned me was hearing Renee describe her and her cats as being "inseparable." Was this type of thinking going to impact our future together? I buried those thoughts in the back of my mind, to be dealt with at a later date. Despite these wonderful stories, I still viewed cats as the "lesser of pets," and I clung to my childhood theory that dogs are better companions.

Imagine my surprise when I discovered that my brother John actually preferred cats over dogs, and that our little brother, Joey, the youngest of eight siblings, had decided to get a feline friend for his daughter. As for our five sisters, they never liked cats, which upended my lifelong belief that cats are for girls.

Meanwhile, my relationship with Renee was progressing to the next stage. It was now time for an overnight trip to New Hampshire to meet her family and the cat that I had heard so much about. Following our arrival and a brief introduction to her parents, Virginia and Bernie, Renee abandoned me for the beautiful, long-haired Arthur, who was standing next to the refrigerator and checking me out from a safe distance. Satisfied that she had given Arthur enough hugs, Renee passed him to me to hold. Photos were taken to record this historic moment. I later tried multiple times to pick up Arthur, but he always stayed six steps away.

The following morning after a restless night on their couch, I saw Arthur make several passes through the living room. He never stopped, and he never took his eyes off of me. That was typical of my interactions with cats. I had never met one that would come near me without someone first handing it to me. And even on those occasions, the cats were not too thrilled.

After that visit, it was obvious that Renee loved and adored cats, and she continued to talk about getting her own someday. I did not want to ruin her dream quite yet, as my plans included only the two of us. No pets.

Back in Boston, we continued to enjoy our frequent walks around the Charles River, Castle Island, and Revere Beach, and after six years together, we knew the direction our lives were heading. Engagement and marriage were on the horizon, life was wonderful, and then everything got that much better.

Renee came home from work one evening and explained that she was going to volunteer one night each week to care for cats at the local animal shelter. I was thrilled and very supportive, believing that this would satisfy her feline desires. Now she could spend time with many different cats every week. As for getting our own feline, I admittedly made some vague promises during those years of courtship, perhaps hoping that she would eventually forget. Sadly, she has a penchant for remembering "everything."

With promises made, how could I change my mind now? Imagine what would have happened to St. Matthew if he had told Jesus that he enjoyed following him around Galilee for three years, but he really missed his old tax-collecting job and wanted to return to his former occupation. I think Jesus would be more forgiving of me than Renee would be.

My false sincerity for wanting a cat masked a secret that I did not share with Renee. Our apartment complex had a "no pets" policy, and I knew that we were not about to move from such a great location in Boston. Yet despite my smugness, life often throws curveballs that we never see coming.

FOUR

Cat named Peter

IN JANUARY OF 2005, Renee and I rode the Amtrak train from Boston to Philadelphia for the weekend to attend a baby shower and to visit the city's famous landmarks. After seeing the Liberty Bell and the U.S. Mint, we happened upon a restaurant called "Rotten Ralph's," an iconic dining establishment. I especially liked its outdoor sign and took several photos.

"What a great name," I remarked to Renee. "If we ever *had* to get a cat, we should name him Ralph." I was in a particularly good mood that afternoon, never expecting much from my comment and forgetting all about it, until nearly seven years later.

DURING THE SUMMER of 2008, a male orange tabby of unknown origin was born in the vicinity of Delavan, Wisconsin, a mostly rural area 60 miles southeast of Madison. Around that same time, a thousand miles away in Boston, Renee and I were a year away from getting married and completely unaware that we would be moving to Wisconsin much sooner than I expected.

There was certainly no brilliant star in the sky to herald that in three years' time, my life would intersect with this stray cat that currently lived halfway across the country. It was incomprehensible.

On a Saturday afternoon in mid-April of 2009, a premature heat wave struck Boston on the day that Renee and I stood in the Boston Public Garden to exchange our marriage vows. Following a six-day honeymoon in Hawaii, we settled back to work while enjoying weekend day-trips throughout New England, until some unexpected news dramatically altered our lives.

Due to a further downturn in the printing and publishing industries, my company announced another round of voluntary layoffs, available to all employees. After considering our options, Renee and I decided I should accept the early-retirement package, and she would leave her current job at Candlewick Press. With our apartment lease about to expire, we would move to Madison, Wisconsin, into my fully remodeled house that I had been renting out to tenants for the previous 14 years.

This sudden change was a life-altering event for Renee. She had never lived away from her beloved East Coast. But on a positive note, the move sparked another of her dreams of finally getting her own cat.

Following our one-way flight to Madison in February of 2010, we were greeted by a brutal Wisconsin winter, much worse than anything Renee had ever experienced. And while Boston is known as the most walkable large city in the country, along with its excellent public transportation, Madison is dominated by commuter car traffic. There is no subway or commuter rail system. You essentially need a car to get anywhere, and Renee does not drive. Fortunately, our residence is in a prime location, one mile from the city center between two lakes—but it is still not the ocean.

The next 18 months proved to be a challenging adjustment for Renee. Since we had mutually decided long ago that we would not have children, her fervent desire for a cat became much more important. Considering the huge sacrifice she made to move halfway across the country, I could not say "no" any longer.

In early October of 2011, Renee and I drove to the Dane County Humane Society in Madison to look for a cat. This was a new experience for me, my first time in an animal shelter. As we entered the building, we were directed down the hall to a viewing area with double-decker rows of cages. The first cage housed three adorable kittens that had stopped their frolicking to stare back at us. I was immediately smitten by what I felt was a "harmless one," until Renee pointed to the note on the glass window, "Adoption pending." After making our way down the hall, I sensed this was not going to be easy.

Some cages were empty, while others were draped with blankets to calm those inside.

Renee had been brimming with excitement when we first arrived, but now she was aware that I was quickly losing my enthusiasm. She had kindly deferred the cat-picking to me, knowing that any cat I selected would be fine with her. Yet her biggest fear was that my criteria would be so stringent that no cat would meet my ever-shifting requirements.

As we moved around the corner to the next viewing area, we saw more cats. According to my benchmarks, many were too young, several too old, one too playful, one too big, one too small, one too plain—but the last one, to both our delights, was just perfect. This two-year-old, black and gray striped male with a beautiful coat of long, silky hair looked wonderful.

We alerted a staff person who escorted us to another room. After we were comfortably seated, she brought in this handsome, fluffy cat and placed him on the floor directly in front of us. He immediately walked away to the opposite side of the room, having no desire or curiosity to interact with us. Even after the staff person repeatedly tried to coax him back our way, he had no interest whatsoever. We even picked him up to no avail. He simply did not like us.

Renee concealed her disappointment, while commenting what a beautiful cat he was, and then she said to the staff person, "We'll think about it." She knew we were not coming back, explaining to me afterward, "I don't want a cat that doesn't want to be with me." We both agreed that we wanted a "buddy cat," one who would very much enjoy being with us forever.

After returning home that day, deflated and depressed, Renee sensed that her chances for adopting a feline friend were quickly diminishing. We had already missed out on one possibility. Several months earlier, a small-framed, all-black female cat started roaming through our back yard and hanging out in our garden for weeks. She did not have a collar, and we had no idea if she even had an owner, so Renee named her "Mikki."

We started feeding Mikki, prompting her to become a regular visitor, often lounging for hours on the stoop by our back door. Renee took every opportunity to pet her, even picking her up and holding her. "I think she wants to be with us," she explained, and I took that as a hint. A few days later, I woke Renee up and told her to hurry down to our living room. Relaxing on the couch was little Mikki who had followed me into the house after I came home from an early errand.

Renee was thrilled; her wish had finally come true. She finally had a cat. Almost.

After only a few minutes of sitting next to Renee, Mikki jumped onto the floor and went directly to our back door. She enjoyed her brief visit, but she did not want to stay inside any longer. She was obviously an outdoor cat. Then Renee's dreams were crushed after I made some inquiries. I discovered that Mikki actually had a real home, only two houses away from ours, and that her real name was "Millie." But we continued to call her Mikki, and she visited quite often and became our good friend, except that she wasn't really *our* cat.

Following our failed attempts at adopting our own cat, Renee's spirits were sinking. She definitely needed something to rekindle her hopes, so I suggested we take a four-mile drive to PetSmart to look at cats available for adoption. I was not expecting much, and neither was Renee. We just wanted to browse, but once we arrived, she was not as surprised as I was.

From twenty feet away, through the glass window of the cat room, I spotted a medium-sized orange cat curled up and asleep in a bottom cage, farthest from the door.

"Wow... I want to see that one," I said as I rushed by all the other cages, going directly to the last one. After a quick glance, I sought out an employee to unlock the cage. Once the door was opened, this cat named Peter stood up, stretched, and casually walked out, stopping by our feet.

"Feel free to pick him up," the employee said.

Renee wanted me to go first, knowing that I had never been able to pick up a cat that had not been handed to me. This was a test. To her utter surprise, and to my delight, Peter let me pick him up. As I held him close to my chest, he immediately turned on his "motor," emitting non-stop purrs. After handing him off to Renee, she held him even closer and did not want to put him down. His purrs never let up.

My only comment: "What a docile, friendly cat."

The description on the cage listed him as "Peter, 3 years old, neutered male, brought to the shelter as a stray." There was no other information, except that he had been at the Lakeland Animal Shelter in Delavan for three months before being transferred to PetSmart a week earlier. Such a vague history triggered warning signs. What's wrong with him? If he was so nice, why wasn't he adopted already? Maybe he's sick?

Despite my excessive caution, I really was smitten with him. He fit my superficial criteria of being "orange," while there was something else that I never would have expected— those huge saucer-like eyes, so soulful and expressive. When he looked at me, he held his gaze, as though he wanted to say something. Best of all, he actually seemed to like me, and he did not struggle when I picked him up and held him for as long as I wanted. I was so thrilled. After a mere five minutes, I simply blurted out, "This is the one."

There was no need to consult Renee. I already knew she was on board. I could see it in her eyes. She later explained that she loved him at first sight, and that she had been holding her breath and hoping that Peter and I would get along. At this point, I was ready to pick him up, carry him to the check-out register, and go directly home. I was not aware that the adoption process was so complicated.

After handing me an adoption application, the employee patiently explained that the completed form needed to be faxed to the shelter for approval, which could take 24 hours. Before Renee could stop me, I asked, "Can't we just take him home today?"

Sensing my frustration, the employee politely gave me a brief tutorial about how shelters always want to be certain that potential adopters are "qualified." That made perfect sense, and I knew this would not be a problem for us. We lived in our own house, we had no debt, no overdue bills, and no outstanding warrants. I started smiling again until she mentioned that they also had to verify that no one else had placed an adoption request for Peter ahead of us.

Now the anxiety was back. I asked if she could immediately call to inquire. She said, "No, you will have to wait for them to contact you." That was a punch in the gut. I had actually found a cat, and we liked each other. If we lost him to someone else, I worried that we would never find another one like him.

After completing the application, we drove home, ate dinner, watched TV, and went to bed. It was a long night, and I was expecting the worst. The next morning, I collided into Renee every time the phone rang. As noon approached, I couldn't wait any longer, so I called the shelter.

"Hello, we were just calling to follow up on our application for a cat." Then I provided our names and the details.

"Oh yes, we were about to call you. Your application for Peter was just approved this morning."

"Thank you so much," I replied in a calm voice while Renee and I were quietly fist-pumping in utter jubilation. Within minutes, we were on our way to PetSmart to pick up Peter. Upon our arrival, I almost crashed through the sliding glass doors as we hurried into the store, corralled an employee, and went directly to the adoption room. Peter was still there, resting in the same spot, as I got down on my knees and looked into the cage. When he saw us, he stretched and pressed his face against the bars.

"What expressive eyes," Renee commented, and then asked him, "Hey, little buddy, are you ready to come with us today?" He did not respond, but he did start purring again.

Our next step was to sign the final adoption form, write out a check for the adoption fee, and buy a $10 cardboard pet carrier. Then I turned to Renee and said, "Time to take 'Ralph' home." He was no longer Peter. His new name was Ralph, just as I had promised seven years earlier. As for Renee, she did not care what I named him, just as long as we actually got a cat. All the way home, she sat in the back seat talking to Ralph, explaining all the fun that awaited him in his new forever home with us.

In hindsight, the process of finding and adopting Ralph ended up being so easy. It was also hard for me to believe that

I disliked cats until Renee's missionary zeal converted me into becoming a cat lover. Despite my newfound interest in felines, I seriously had no idea whatsoever about the chaotic mess that I had just gotten myself into.

FIVE

Return policy

IN 2006, WHILE hiking the hilly trail that links the five coastal cities of Cinque Terre in northwest Italy, Renee and I made a brief stop for a glass of fresh-squeezed orange juice. Seated on a public bench under the shade of an olive tree, I was too preoccupied with the view to realize that a stray orange cat had joined me on the other end of the bench. I wouldn't have noticed if Renee had not pointed it out. This was the first time that a cat had approached me and not run away, perhaps because I was sitting in its spot.

A full decade later, Renee showed me the photo that she had taken of me and that orange cat sitting together in Italy. I was surprised and stunned. It looked remarkably like Ralph, and that was six years before Ralph came into our lives.

After a life-long dislike of cats and a preference for dogs, I had finally succumbed to getting a cat. Driving home from PetSmart, I could hear Renee in the back seat talking nonstop to Ralph. She could hardly contain her excitement, having finally fulfilled her lifelong dream of having her own cat. This was undoubtedly the happiest day of her life.

With my eyes on the traffic, I was unsure I could even remember what Ralph looked like, but he was real, and he was now "our cat." I also had time to process powerful new emotions of elation, satisfaction, victory, relief, second-guessing, and even a touch of dread. My initial thought was that I had won the feline lottery. Ralph was a nice-looking cat. However, the euphoria was wearing off quickly, and I was beginning to feel a bit queasy and nauseous. I questioned my judgment and my decision. What the heck had I just done? Was this really all about pleasing Renee? Unlike buying a new car, this cat was a living thing that we had to take care of forever.

Newly retired, I sensed my dreams of world travel had just been permanently altered. Who would babysit this cat? And how could we ever go away on vacation again?

Meanwhile, the one-way conversation in the back seat continued. Renee whispered to me that she was peeking into the top of the cardboard carrier to pet Ralph on the head, while also reassuring him that his new home would be wonderful. He responded with a simple "meow."

The walk from our detached garage to the back door is 24 feet. Renee walked slowly, clutching her precious cargo as though she were holding nitroglycerin. Once inside, she cautiously walked up the five steps to the hallway and gently put the box on the floor. Carefully lifting him out, she set him free to explore his new two-story home. Ralph appeared a bit dazed as he studied his surroundings and then cautiously wandered from room to room: kitchen, dining room, living room, and finally stopping by the floor lamp near the front door. And then my worst fears took hold.

"Chomp, chomp, chomp." He started to bite on the lamp cord!

"No, Ralph... no, no, no!" I shouted.

I hastened across the room, gently placing my hands on his mid-section and rotating him 180 degrees toward the dining room. He was not interested, preferring instead to go to our stereo system and start chewing on the thin speaker wires and the electrical plug.

"No, Ralph, no! Bad cat... bad, bad, bad," I said, but he was still not listening.

After I bent down to redirect him, his ignition switch kicked in, and he bolted full speed through the dining room, down the hallway, and into our TV room, directly to another lamp cord. "Chomp, chomp." I stopped him again, while he continued snapping his jaws like a crocodile. "Geeeeez, Ralph. No, no, no." Then I started calling out for Renee. "What are we going to do?"

I felt certain that she could handle the situation, but I was taken aback by her response. "Cats will be cats, and they will do want they want to do." She was not troubled, but I was hysterical. I felt certain that Ralph was going to be electrocuted or get a serious burn if he actually bit through one of those 110-volt wires. Even if the wall switch was not turned on, he was still damaging the cords. I recalled an old Chevy Chase holiday movie in which a cat bit into the Christmas tree lights, and "zappppp." It was funny then, but not now.

As Ralph's antics continued, Renee became concerned, but more about me than him. She hoped that after a brief interlude, Ralph and I would both settle down. To help out, she distracted him with a generously filled bowl of kibble.

"Chomp, chomp, chomp." These "chomps" were music to my ears since they involved food, not electrical wires. But after a few mouthfuls, he was again racing across the room, straight back to the lamp cord, and I was becoming unhinged. "Reneeeeee..."

This time, she picked him up and carried him to the sofa in the TV room, where she sat petting him. He seemed to enjoy the attention for a short time, but then jumped to the floor and ran back to the living room and the other lamp cord. His teething days were over, so why the sudden fascination with biting cords? These episodes were only a warm-up for what lay ahead.

Renee firmly suggested that I needed to calm down and relax, reminding me again, "He's just a cat." She said it would be helpful if I refocused my energy and prepared his litter box. I suggested placing it in the dining room, but Renee vetoed that as too unsightly. I then suggested the landing by the back door, but being next to the stairs, that was deemed too dangerous. The only other option was the basement. After positioning his new box at the bottom of the basement stairs and filling it with litter, I called to Renee to bring the boy downstairs so we could introduce him to his "poop box."

Once his four paws made contact with the litter, he sniffed around, but showed no interest. Instead, he stepped out of the box and took off running toward the back of the basement, a virtual cat's playground with a dozen large storage shelves, three workbenches, sawhorses, an industrial table saw, air compressor, coils of electrical wire, paint cans, and plumbing pipes. In the far corner were stacks of lumber and plywood. Another area was dedicated to pneumatic nail guns, jig saws, circular saws, a router, a planer, and drills. Most of these power tools had cords.

The workshop takes up 90 percent of the basement, resembling a Home Depot annex. For a cat running loose, this is an extremely dangerous playground. When Ralph jumped up on my table saw, nearly landing on the ten-inch, 60-tooth carbide blade, I shouted to Renee for help. We both chased him around the entire basement for 15 minutes until he finally allowed us to catch him. After Renee carried Ralph upstairs, he immediately returned to biting lamp cords and then chewed on my USB cables, ensuring they would never again transfer data.

That was the tipping point. I grabbed my wallet and car keys, and headed out the door. Renee knew I was extremely upset and did not try to stop me. As I drove down the street in no particular direction, I started screaming as loudly as I could, with the windows rolled up, cursing myself for making a stupid decision that I'd certainly regret for the rest of my life. Our house, which I spent many years remodeling, was about to be wrecked by a destructive cat, one we should never have adopted. "Why, why, why?" I kept repeating.

My retirement dreams were definitely crushed. I should have talked Renee into volunteering at a shelter. Or perhaps we should have moved to Europe for a year to some rustic village distracting enough to make her forget about cats. As my mind swirled with anger, remorse, and frustration, I turned the car around and drove back to PetSmart. Once inside, I went directly to a store manager, taking deep breaths while regaining some semblance of composure.

"Excuse me," I said, in as calm a tone as I could manage, "I just want to inquire about this cat that we adopted earlier today." I paused for a moment, then continued, "I believe we have a huge problem with him. He's tearing up our house, and perhaps he really isn't the best fit for us. We may have been too hasty in adopting him."

The manager appeared quite empathetic and responded, "Oh... I'm so sorry to hear that." And then he said, "Unfortunately, there's nothing I can do to help. It's out of our hands. You'll have to contact the shelter and work it out with them."

"Oh great," I thought while I continued to stand there, waiting for him to change his mind or perhaps hoping we could find some common ground.

"Sorry," he said again. "I just hope you can work something out with the shelter." Then he turned and walked away leaving me in a quandary.

Did he not know the shelter was 75 miles away?

As I left the store, I called my friend Walter in Boston. Judging by my tone, he thought someone had just died. Walter and his wife, Sarah, are both cat lovers, and they have two of their own. After explaining my dilemma and expecting that his sage-like wisdom and advice would solve my problem, I was mistaken.

"Settle down, big guy. Don't be so nervous. Give the *boy* a chance. He's a cat. Let him get used to you." Walter was really no help at all.

Since that was not what I wanted to hear, I called my

brother John, but he had more empathy for Ralph than for his own brother. Five minutes later, I slowly pulled into our garage, hesitating to go back inside the house. I even contemplated staying outside to mow the lawn, which did not need mowing. Considering that Ralph had been in our home for less than a day, I started wondering what new destruction he had caused while I was away.

I was astonished to find Renee and Ralph calmly sitting on the couch in the TV room. They looked so peaceful together. Perhaps he was out of energy and just taking a breather before launching his next assault. Even though Renee appeared relaxed and calm, I sensed that she was extremely nervous, worrying that Ralph would not be staying with us for much longer. When I mentioned that I had gone back to PetSmart, she started crying and got off the couch, leaving me alone in the room with Ralph.

This little orange terror remained on the couch, stretching out lengthwise on his side and facing me with a look of innocence. I had to admit he was handsome and cute, so I knelt down in front of him and buried my face directly in his exposed underbelly. His furry hair smelled so good.

"Ralph, Ralph, Ralph. Why can't you be a good boy? Please be good. I don't want to take you back. We want you to stay; we really do. So please, please be good." And then I smothered him with another hug. He did not budge, not even a tiny bit, but he did turn on what we would later call his "Jurassic purr."

I did settle down, perhaps feeling a bit embarrassed that I may have overreacted "just a little." However, I had no way of knowing that he was toying with me, and that his idea of having fun was just beginning.

Years later, Renee would reflect back on that first day when she had been sad and very concerned that I was actually going to return Ralph to the shelter. She had purposely left me alone with him in the TV room as a last resort, hoping it would spark even the slightest connection between us. At the time, I had no idea she had been quietly watching me from the doorway and struggling to hold back the tears when she saw me on my knees whispering to Ralph. She admitted it was the most touching sight she had ever witnessed.

Clinging to a glimmer of hope after seeing me hugging Ralph and talking to him, Renee believed that "feline magic" had finally taken ahold of me. She was indeed correct, but her sense of timing was premature.

Meanwhile, Ralph's bathroom habits became an immediate issue. Obviously a finicky cat, we had to offer him three different-sized boxes to determine which he preferred. What should have been an easy decision for him was not. He tested all three. The first was too small, the second too tall, and the third too big. He chose a fourth option. He wanted *two* litter boxes: the small one for peeing and the big one for pooping, and he actually used them accordingly.

The largest was a plastic rectangular storage bin, three feet long and only six inches high, originally designed to slide under beds or stack on shelves. With its rounded edges, it was perfect to accommodate Ralph's unusual manner of pooping, and Renee admitted she had never seen any cat perform so adroitly.

With all four paws nearly touching each other, Ralph balanced himself perfectly on the top rim of one corner, lifting his furry tail high while making a deposit. When he tried that acrobatic move in the small box, his weight on the rim tipped the whole box over on top of him. He found the big storage box to be much sturdier. Its size, combined with the added weight from more litter, ensured that it would never move or tip.

I found his balancing-on-the-box routine to be so unusual that I wanted to film it for *America's Funniest Home Videos*, but Renee was against it, insisting Ralph needed his "dignity." I countered, "Why would he care? He has no problem barging into the bathroom to watch me." I was overruled, and we never shot the video, missing out on what I believed would have been a first-place win and a $10,000 prize.

SIX

Barriers and beans

PREMIERING ON THE Animal Planet network in 2011 and running for 11 seasons, the popular cable show *My Cat from Hell* featured Jackson Galaxy, a former musician who became a respected cat behaviorist. The series followed his exploits going into people's homes to resolve horrific problems and behavioral issues of troubled felines. The conflicts he encountered were mind-boggling—owner vs. cat, cat vs. cat, cat vs. neighbor cat, cat vs. child, cat pooping and peeing outside the box, cat attacking owners, cat hating owner's boyfriend, cat terrorizing visitors. Then there was bully cat, mean cat, escape-artist cat, evil cat, blood-thirsty cat, demon cat, fat cat, destructive cat, scary cat, and shy cat.

Jackson did a magnificent job helping and comforting owners and their cats in circumstances that appeared to be untenable and irreversible. He succeeded in most situations, while educating viewers to better understand the complexities and behaviors of their cherished pets.

Renee was thankful that I did not start watching these episodes until *after* we adopted a cat; otherwise, I may have vigorously objected to ever getting one, fearing it might be one of those "cats from hell."

After Ralph's tumultuous first day in our house, Renee wanted to discuss his sleeping arrangements. I was already mentally and emotionally drained, so I really didn't care where he slept. Since he had settled down a bit and seemed comfortable on the living room couch, I suggested we leave him there. After I went upstairs to bed, Renee remained behind to say goodnight.

As I fluffed my pillow, I could hear her soft, soothing voice downstairs talking to Ralph as though he were an infant that she found on our doorstep. A bit later, Renee woke me up, insisting that Ralph should not be sleeping in the dark in an unfamiliar house. He needed some lighting, which meant that I had to get out of bed and go to the basement to find several plug-in nightlights.

Exhausted from the day's events, I slept soundly that night. The last thing I recalled was a happy and content smile on Renee's face. In the morning, she got up early and hustled downstairs, much the way an excited child runs to check for presents under the Christmas tree. She was so happy and enthusiastic to see him still asleep on the couch.

I was still in the bedroom, half-asleep, when I suddenly bolted out of bed and down the stairs to do a thorough inspection of all the electrical cords, hoping they were still intact and not frayed or chewed. Satisfied that the house was not going to burst into flames, I started to relax. My only thrilling moment was discovering that Ralph had found his own way down to the basement at night to use his litter box. What a relief!

Throughout the rest of the day, Renee sat with Ralph while I drove back to PetSmart to shop for a pheromone collar that would supposedly calm him down and ease his fetish for chewing on wires. Unbeknown to Renee, I also had a discussion with a *different* store manager to ask again about their "return policy." He was polite, but the answer was still "no." He said I would have to contact the shelter.

On my way home, I continued to contemplate the extent of how my life had been ruined, so I called my friend, Arnie, who lived in a rural area of the state. I thought he might want another cat. He declined, but he did offer to give me *his* cat.

Meanwhile, I still had serious doubts about Ralph. I calculated that I was within the 48-hour "return window," a policy I had created for myself. And I was mentally preparing to drive him 75 miles to the shelter before Renee's parents showed up the following day for their annual visit. If Ralph remained in our home just one day longer, I felt certain we would be stuck with him permanently, and my retirement dreams for travel and adventure would be dashed forever.

During his second night, with the return-clock ticking down toward zero, my nerves were still frayed, and that was *before* I discovered that my other USB cable was punctured with a hundred tiny holes, and that my desk had been ransacked.

Instead of sleeping on the couch again, Ralph wandered upstairs, circled our bed, and jumped up next to Renee, snuggling tight against her chest. With her arm around him, they both slept soundly through the night. When she awoke, his head was tucked under her chin, and she was thrilled.

I was surprised by this transformation. Renee and Ralph had bonded almost instantly, and they looked incredibly cute together. She also maintained that Ralph was an extraordinary cat. In a moment of sheer weakness and against my better judgment, I decided to commute his probation. Ralph was not going back to the shelter; he would remain with us. I also felt that Ralph and I could reach an "understanding," and I could alter his bad habits. How naive was I?

The third day served up another surprise. Renee's parents, Virginia and Bernie, arrived for their second visit to Wisconsin. Virginia is a huge cat lover, bubbling with enthusiasm when she walked in the back door and saw this fine specimen of an orange cat looking down at her from the top of the stairs. She and Renee immediately took turns pampering the "kid" and taking photos. Ralph become the sole focal point for their entire weeklong stay. As we spent our evenings sitting around and chatting, he never once wandered away from us, always seeking attention from whomever would provide it.

Their visit went by fast, and my in-laws' biggest thrill was not the various sights in Madison, but rather all the fun they had with Ralph: sitting with him, petting him, and giving him treats. After they flew home, Renee and I returned to a bit of normalcy. We also noticed that every time we came back from a walk or an errand, Ralph was always sitting in the window by the back door waiting for us. He looked adorable, but he was also a smart and wily cat, and he knew exactly how to push my buttons.

A few days later, just after dark, Ralph vanished. We couldn't find him anywhere on the first or second floor, so I went down to the basement. Two glowing eyes were staring back at me in the dark. Aside from his litter box, this was definitely *not* a safe area to play.

The basement foundation of our 90-year-old house had been constructed of random stone and clay tile blocks, and remained damp and musty, despite a dehumidifier that ran continuously. The entire basement had no interior walls. This big open space served mostly as a repository for my tools and building supplies, which presented a real danger to any pet. And just as I feared, Ralph loved being in that basement.

Blocking off his litter box area from the rest of the basement was a huge challenge. My initial idea was to adhere a special wire on the concrete floor, separating the two areas. I intended to put a shock-collar around Ralph's neck so that anytime he ventured across the wire, he would get a low-voltage jolt. This technology is commonly used for dogs to train them not to venture outside the boundaries of their yard, but I could not find any information about using it indoors on cats. While it may have been a novel idea, Renee thought it was outright ridiculous, saying that if I was serious, she wanted to put the collar around my neck and test it on me.

I decided to look for another solution, but before I could move forward, Ralph managed to get his new pheromone collar partially off and stuck between his jaws like the bit on a horse. We had to carefully cut the collar off with safety scissors, and then threw the collar in the trash.

As for the basement, the situation was becoming much more serious. Every time Ralph came back upstairs, he was covered in cobwebs and dust, and he would start sneezing.

I spent days vacuuming with little success. The continuously flaking mortar between the stones of the old foundation made my task as challenging as Hercules cleaning the Aegean stables. My efforts also did nothing to mitigate the potential dangers from all my power tools and building supplies.

Ralph's health and safety now started to concern Renee. She agreed that Ralph needed his own dedicated bathroom, so I constructed four new walls at the bottom of the basement stairs. This new seven-by-nine-foot "bathroom," with no plumbing, was perfect for his litter boxes. Painted a bright orange, the room also included a standard 36" door that cut off his access to the rest of the basement. To our surprise, Ralph's only fascination with his bathroom was the new door. He already knew what lay behind it and would sometimes slip past us when the door was inadvertently left open, leading to a lengthy rodeo of cat-wrangling to get him out.

On one such occasion when he gained entry, I found him sitting quietly on our treadmill. After he refused to budge, I turned it on at one mph and watched the belt slowly carry him toward the edge. Only at the last moment did he jump down before being dumped off. I thought it was funny, but I got quite a scolding from Renee for being so mean to "her" cat. She just didn't realize that Ralph seemed to enjoy the ride.

With the basement problem solved, I barely had time to catch my breath before Ralph's behavior spiraled out of control again, especially in the TV room.

Although I had securely taped two empty Kleenex boxes over all the wiring and cables behind the TV, he still liked to explore behind it, until one evening when he started meowing for help. Apparently, both of his hind legs had slipped down between the back of the TV cabinet and the wall, and he was stuck. Renee and I spent several minutes gently extracting him, using our hands like small cranes to lift him out.

I shuddered to think that if he had actually fallen all the way down, it would have been impossible for him to wiggle up and out from such a tight, confined space. This needed an immediate remedy. I drove to the store and purchased more five-foot foam noodles, wedging them between the wall and the TV cabinet to ensure that Ralph would never fall into that deadly crevasse again.

To block off his access to the back of the TV, I placed an imposing two-foot SpongeBob piñata at one end and several empty boxes at the other. He simply pushed them off, repeatedly, so I gave up, but the foam noodles worked so well that I purchased a dozen more, trimming and cutting them to stuff into all sorts of dangerous spaces. "Ralph-proofing" the house remained an ongoing project.

My biggest concern remained Ralph's attraction to electrical cords and cable wires, including plugs and outlets. We were told that using squirt guns could be a good deterrent, but they were not. The only result was a thoroughly wet cat with no impulse control. Renee found a better solution by using flexible plastic cable bundlers that she trimmed and slipped over all the exposed electrical cords throughout the house. As a further deterrent, she smeared cat-repellent paste on them and sprinkled hot pepper flakes onto the gooey paste. Ralph did not like hot and spicy, so all the cords and cables on our lamps, TV, stereo, and computers were now protected.

We thought we won that battle until he started biting on the electrical plugs and finally pulled one completely out of the wall outlet. Renee immediately placed a rush-order for plastic covers that prevent children, or cats, from accessing the outlets. These worked so well that Renee ordered four more.

In a search of more excitement, Ralph turned his attention to the immense, old laser printer on the file cabinet next to my desk. He couldn't resist. Despite the printer being capped with rolls of paper towels and an empty box, there remained a narrow gap, only four inches wide, that plunged five feet to the floor, between the cabinet and the wall. If Ralph fell, he would not be able to get out.

One afternoon, I saw Ralph climb to the top and start to slide down, about to disappear behind the cabinet. I quickly caught him before he harmed or injured himself. He didn't object because he knew he was in serious trouble. But that did not stop him from further explorations.

My solution was to cut a piece of plywood and place it on top of the file cabinet, effectively sealing off the open spaces in that corner of the room. I then jammed ten rolls of toilet paper and several more rolls of paper towels around the sides of the printer. All the crevices were filled so tightly that even a mouse could not squeeze past.

Renee always watched me in amusement, never commenting. She knew it was like holding water in your hand and watching it leak out between your fingers. And just as I was feeling more confident about curing Ralph's bad behavior, he decided he wanted to start making phone calls.

"Reneeeeee," I shouted, "Please come and get your cat." Although I had already taped the charging station to my desk, Ralph discovered how much fun it was to slap the telephone handset out of its stand and then chew on the charging cord.

On my next trip to the grocery store, I purchased 10 one-pound bags of dried, white beans—I called them "sandbags"—which I stacked against the phone and charging station, and on top of all the exposed low-voltage wires. As I was layering these bags of beans, I did not realize that Ralph was lying on the desk watching me. Once my sandbagging was complete, he immediately started digging a trench through those bags, prompting me to call out to Renee, "We're going to need a lot more beans."

I later wondered what the cashier at the grocery store thought when my only purchase was 10 more bags of dried beans and nothing else. As for my beautiful oak desk, it was now overwhelmingly cluttered and disgusting. Ralph essentially drove me away from my desk, rendering it fairly useless as a work area, until Renee very calmly solved the problem.

"Just close the door," she said. What a great, simple idea. I took her advice, but I was dealing with no ordinary cat.

In late February, I started assembling all my tax receipts and statements, spreading them across the few uncluttered areas of my desk and on top of the bags of beans. For several hours, Ralph stationed himself outside the door, performing a symphony of long, drawn-out "meows."

Renee chastised me from the hallway. "Don't you hear those *sad* meows? He wants to be in there with you."

I felt guilty and ashamed. Ralph really did sound so sad, and maybe he really did miss me, but that was my mistake when I fell for his Trojan Cat routine. As soon as I yelled to Renee, "Release the Kraken!" she opened the door, and Ralph ran directly to my desk. In a single leap, he landed on neatly piled stacks of tax forms, crumpling half of them while scattering all the rest onto the floor.

I called out for help, "Reneeeeee."

She quickly ran in and scooped him off my desk. "Be nice," she said, referring to me, since Ralph could apparently do no wrong. After closing the door again, I could hear her comforting him as they sat in the living room. But fifteen minutes later, Ralph was outside the door again, this time opting for show tunes with his rendition of "Cat on a Hot Tin Roof."

"Me-oooooooow, meeee-ow, me-oooooooow."

My concentration was destroyed, but until all my tax forms were completed, there would be "no admittance."

As the months rolled by, Ralph did settle down, allowing his cuteness to captivate us—until our wireless service suddenly quit functioning. I tried unsuccessfully for two hours to resolve the problem and then contacted our neighbor, Zach, a computer tech specialist at the University of Wisconsin. He stopped by after work and spent an hour troubleshooting our system, from one possibility to another.

Finally, in one of those "ahhhh" moments, Zach reached behind the wireless router and pushed the "on" button. That was when I turned and looked at Ralph, sitting nearby inquisitively watching us. Earlier that day, I remembered seeing him on my desk swatting and biting on the router's antennas. Somehow, he managed to reach around and tap the power button.

In order to cat-proof the router, I re-purposed a 12" x 18" heavy-duty box by cutting the flaps and placing it upside down over the router. I weighed it down with a four-pound coffee table book about the Roman Empire, ensuring that Caesar's legions would hold off an invasion from the "Orange barbarian." Of course, Ralph was sitting on the desk watching me the whole time.

Once I had safely covered the router, Ralph used the box as a step stool to extend his paw up the wall and knock down my favorite oil painting, a sentimental piece of art, despite its $10 value. I just shook my head and went directly to the basement for a hammer and a much larger nail. As soon as I had rehung the painting on the wall, he had another go at it, unsuccessfully—but he did manage to tilt it about 15 degrees, and that was how it would remain.

Although I now spent considerably less time at my desk, it was at least *secure*, just as long as I remembered to stay alert and not become complacent.

On one occasion when I briefly left the room, I returned to discover that Ralph was sitting inside the top desk drawer using his jaws and paws to empty all of the contents—pens, markers, a pencil sharper, old watches, business cards, a letter opener, and many small notebooks. Most of it was now on the floor. The closer I got to him, the faster he dug. Instead of chasing him away, I put my face as far into the drawer as possible. He did, too. Together we examined what few items still remained. After he and I were satisfied he had done a thorough job, he jumped out of the drawer and went to the kitchen to reward himself with some kibble. When he returned, he found the desk drawer closed... forever.

SEVEN

Ding dong... visitors

ALTHOUGH THERE ARE many anecdotal stories about cats waking people up at night, I felt Ralph was the exception because he slept in bed with us throughout the night and did not stir until after 7 a.m. However, after only one week, that changed when he began waking up earlier than a rooster. To help me understand, Renee introduced me to a new word—crepuscular.

I initially thought it was a disease, until Renee explained it was a proper and well-accepted description of feline behavior, meaning that cats are most active during the twilight and pre-dawn hours of the day. If she had told me that ahead of time, I would have chosen a "non-crepuscular" cat, or perhaps a dog.

AS A YOUNGSTER, my favorite Saturday morning TV cartoon show was *Rocky and Bullwinkle*. With his signature leather cap and goggles, Rocky was an energetic flying squirrel, with Bullwinkle, the moose, as his sidekick and best friend. I never imaged that 55 years later I would have my own Rocky, the flying cat.

Watching Ralph race down the second-floor carpeted stairs reminded me of a flying squirrel. Airborne at full throttle, he soared completely over the last three steps with all four paws extended outward like the landing gear of a Boeing jet. He never crash-landed, always touching down smoothly with a gentle thud and sliding to a complete stop on the hardwood floor. He then turned 90 degrees toward the kitchen and taxied over to his food bowl to refuel.

In hindsight, I should have named him Rocky, considering that one of my boyhood nicknames was Moose... although in the cartoon, the squirrel was the brains of the duo, a telling sign of what lay ahead for me.

AS I ROUNDED the corner into the dining room, I almost walked past a most unusual sight. Ralph was dangling precariously on our wooden wine rack, quiet and still, almost as though I caught him in the act of trying to uncork a very fine Bordeaux. Then I realized he was actually stuck there.

His front paws were entangled in the top wooden slats, while the rest of his body hung down like a slab of meat at the butcher shop. Fortunately, his rear paws were delicately balancing his body on the neck of a five-dollar bottle of red wine from Trader Joe's. I had no idea how long he had been hanging there, but he seemed very relieved when I helped him off the rack. Never again did he try to select another vintage. Regular tap water would remain his beverage of choice.

AFTER RALPH'S PREDICAMENT with the wine rack, he avoided it permanently. However, one morning as I passed through the dining room and turned into the kitchen, I stopped abruptly when I saw Ralph plastered against the oven door of our gas stove. His front paws were stretched upward and lodged under the heavy iron grate of the gas stovetop, while his body was fully extended downward with his rear paws balanced on the narrow rim of the stove's storage drawer below. He looked like a cat that was being tortured on the rack during the Inquisition.

I stood there for a moment, shaking my head in disbelief. After I helped him down, along with several words of admonishment, he acted like it was no big deal and then wandered over to his empty food bowl expecting immediate replenishment. I later explained this incident to Renee, but she thought I was exaggerating. Why was I the only one to witness such bad behavior? I told Renee that if Ralph tried that again, I would leave him hanging, to which she responded, "Not unless you want to move into the neighbor's dog house."

I HAD JUST poured milk on my cereal and sat down at the dining room table with the morning newspaper. Ralph got up from his nearby window perch, stepped across to the table, and went directly to my bowl of Cheerios. The taste of oats was not to his liking, but the milk was.

As I raised the first spoonful to my mouth, he stared at me with that "where's mine?" look. As I dug deep for a second spoonful, he moved closer to my bowl, partially blocking the newspaper. In order to continue reading, I lifted his tail with my left hand while spooning cereal with my right. Then he moved again, now lying across the entire paper and not budging. I got up, leaving my cereal to drown, and went to the kitchen to get his tasty tuna treats. After I set a handful at the end of the table, as far away from my newspaper as possible, he got up slowly and smugly, probably thinking, "Was that so hard?"

A minute later, as I was about to enjoy my delicious glazed donut, I noticed something odd. It had bite-marks all over it. "Thanks a lot, Ralph..."

A few weeks after Renee's parents made their annual visit, my sister Judy became the first member of my family to meet Ralph. As soon as she rang our doorbell, Ralph snapped out of a catnap on his window perch and raced to the front door to greet her. Once inside, Judy made herself comfortable on the living room couch. Ralph jumped up and laid firmly by her side and, shockingly, *not* next to us. That was pretty bold of Ralph for a first-time meeting. He even rested his paw on Judy's thigh, perhaps to remind her of his presence.

As the three of us began chatting, Judy reached out and started petting Ralph on his head. She also glanced down and commented, "Gee, he is so friendly. You two are really lucky to have such a nice cat." If only she knew.

Because her visit was brief, I did not want to waste precious time focusing on all of Ralph's bad behaviors, so I steered the conversation to other matters and ushered her into the kitchen for a glass of water. Ralph followed Judy from room to room, even returning to sit next to her on the couch. Twenty minutes later, they both got up; she had to leave for her nightshift at the hospital, while Ralph went to the kitchen for some kibble. As Judy turned to say good-bye, she and Ralph made eye contact from three rooms away. In an impulsive move, she ducked down behind the couch, peeked out at Ralph, and then hid again. The game was on.

Ralph forgot about food and quickly hustled back to the living room in search of his new friend. He and Judy played several rounds of hide-and-seek, with Ralph always rewarding her with head butts. Despite the fun, Judy finally had to leave. As she drove away, Renee and I marveled at Ralph's sociability and the interaction between him and Judy.

Admittedly, I was a bit jealous that I had not thought up this game of hide-and-seek after seeing Ralph be so playful. But it would still take me nearly a year to comprehend that Ralph's actions that day were just part of his normal, extroverted behavior, and that he genuinely liked everyone.

Ralph had several more interactions with strangers over

the following weeks. Most went exceedingly well; two were not so good.

Our first overnight guest, Katie, a former business associate, happened to be passing through Madison and was unable to find a hotel room. We offered her our sleeper sofa, but she chose the couch since she had an early morning flight. Sometime before dawn, she woke up and saw Ralph sitting on the arm of the overstuffed couch, just inches from her head, intently looking down at her. Katie admitted she was initially startled, but then realized it was a pleasant good-morning surprise. Ralph was just curious and friendly, even with a total stranger like Katie.

Our next overnight guest and longtime friend, John, drove to Madison to spend the day visiting his mother, and later joined us for dinner and slept on our sleeper sofa. The next morning, John explained that throughout the night he felt a "lump" against his back as he laid on his side. Every time he moved away, even just a little bit, the lump moved with him. John thought it was quite funny, adding that he had almost shifted himself completely off the mattress.

We had no idea of Ralph's trip downstairs to snug with John because when we woke up, Ralph was sound asleep under Renee's chin. This is just another example of how much Ralph loved to interact with total strangers. However, not everyone likes felines, and that soon became evident.

When a friend from college stopped by for a brief visit, Ralph stepped forward to say "meow," but she was not thrilled to meet him. And as we were touring our house, she turned around and looked at Ralph, and then said to us, "Why is *it* following me?" Moments later, she excused herself to use the bathroom, the one with the faulty lock on the door that I was always promising to fix. When I heard a shriek, I was certain that Ralph had pushed the door open and gone inside. Then a voice yelled, "Hey, you, get out of here!"

Ralph immediately scampered out of the bathroom, while she just as quickly announced that her visit had concluded. She definitely did not like cats, but it certainly didn't bother Ralph. The incident also confirmed that Ralph thoroughly enjoyed being around and interacting with everyone.

Around that same time period, a technician came to our house to adjust the fan speed on our new furnace. As he sat on the basement floor studying an electrical schematic, Ralph kept climbing onto his lap in a cute and friendly manner. This could have been a Norman Rockwell scene, except the technician was not amused and forcibly shoved Ralph aside twice. Before I could intervene, Renee rushed to the basement and carried Ralph back upstairs. The whole incident upset us more than it bothered Ralph.

The only time Ralph had trouble interacting was when a group of my sisters and nieces stopped by for a summertime visit. With all eight of us tightly gathered on the front porch, there was scant room for a little guy like Ralph. He had to carefully navigate among the many pairs of legs and feet, ultimately choosing to lie down directly underneath a rattan rocking chair that was now occupied. As Ralph's tail swayed back and forth from under the curved rocking rails, my anxiety soared. All I could imagine was Edgar Allan Poe's "The Pit and the Pendulum," expecting to hear a cat-curdling scream at any moment.

Renee also recognized the danger. She nonchalantly stood up and walked behind the rocking chair, scooping him up and bringing him back to the couch where she placed him next to her. No one even noticed. After everyone had departed, I immediately dragged the rocking chair off the porch, put it in the back of our SUV, and later gifted it to my sister Jean, who told us to thank Ralph again. Only a few months earlier, Ralph was responsible for giving Jean our new wicker loveseat that he disliked because there was not enough room for all three of us. That meant an upgrade to a full-size outdoor couch, an expense we could have avoided if we did not have a cat.

Meanwhile, Ralph's need to socialize never abated. No matter where he was in the house, the "ding-dong" from the doorbell triggered a Pavlovian response, causing him to race to the front door, always ahead of Renee or me. After ushering guests into the living room, Ralph always chose to sit next to them and *not* with us. If any visit dragged on too long, he would lay his head down next to them and take a nap, while resting a paw on their arm or thigh. He was a very touchy-feely type of cat.

Within the first year, all of our one-time and repeat visitors were making similar observations about Ralph's social behavior. Several dog owners pointed out that he acted more like a canine than a feline. Even people who had their own cats were genuinely awed by Ralph's extroverted personality and his desire to always interact with them.

"Was he a circus cat?" someone quipped.

Ralph had become quite the goodwill ambassador for his *Felis domesticus* species, and when coupled with his cuteness, affection, and endearing behavior toward others, people would not believe that he had a dark side.

For whatever reason, as soon as our guests had departed,

Ralph would act up and torment me with various misdeeds. I sensed that even Jackson Galaxy would have been perplexed. And, of course, it was entirely possible that my ignorance of cats, their characteristics, and their natural behavior led me down this dark path. People would often tell me that cats are trainable, while others would insist that cats will eventually settle down in their new home. I had yet to be convinced because I had no past experience to judge or compare what I perceived as bad behavior.

And then one afternoon, I had the first of many epiphanies. The doorbell rang and Ralph jumped off the couch and raced to the door. It was a package delivery, no visitors. Before opening the door, I looked down and observed Ralph patiently standing next to me. At that moment, I was acutely aware that he feared no one and loved everyone, no matter who they were. He simply had this insatiable desire to interact with everyone.

Having been surrounded by cats all her life, Renee admitted years later that she knew from Ralph's very first day with us that his sociability was highly unusual, far exceeding any cat that she had ever encountered. As for Ralph, he continued to charm many more family members, friends, and strangers who complimented him for his friendliness, boldness, and good looks.

I often said that Ralph used his big personality to mask all the bad stuff he did, perhaps being the feline version of Jekyll and Hyde. But with Renee always defending him, my only defense is to provide a full, in-depth explanation, detailing his disruptive behaviors throughout our house—room by room—without any exaggeration.

EIGHT

Who needs sleep?

ONE EVENING AS I was sitting at my desk paying some bills, Ralph slowly got off the couch and jumped on the desk to watch. After I repeatedly ignored him, he lowered his head and gently bit into my forearm without breaking the skin. After about ten seconds, he let go and stared up at me. I then bent down, lifted his front leg up to my mouth, and bit it for even longer using my gums instead of my teeth to ensure I would not inflict any damage.

Ralph was stunned. After contemplating this for a moment, he gently bit me again, this time for even longer. Not to be outdone, I bit him back a second time, and after another of these exchanges, we called a truce. He went back to the couch to nap, and I resumed paying bills, while Renee shook her head in disbelief, wondering if he and I could act any more childish or immature.

I OFTEN LIKE to take a newspaper or magazine into the bathroom to relax for a few minutes and read without interruption. On one occasion, Ralph pushed the door open and casually strolled in, jumping up on the bathroom vanity and walking to the end of the counter, next to where I was sitting. He just wanted to see what I was doing.

After Ralph placed his front paw on my shoulder, I must have moved slightly because he lost his balance and fell through the center of my newspaper, leaving a hole the size of a cannonball and getting himself tangled in my boxer shorts. He somehow managed to climb out and was unharmed but a bit fazed. Unfortunately, he never stopped bothering me in the bathroom, until I finally fixed the latch on the door.

ON HIS CAGE at PetSmart, the shelter listed Ralph's description as "medium hair," but after many months of a healthy diet in a stable environment, his hair more than doubled in length. It became so long that I suggested we spray Pledge on his underside and let him walk around the house dusting the hardwood floors. I wasn't serious, but it was funny during the cold, dry winter to see Ralph's hair standing straight out from his body, as if he had just stuck his paw in an electrical socket. He looked like a giant puff ball, which prompted Renee to give him one of his early nicknames: "Puffle."

If Jackson Galaxy were to examine Ralph's bad behavior, the first place to start would be our upstairs bedroom.

Since Renee and I are perpetual night owls, we typically go upstairs to bed around 11:00 p.m. and read books until well past midnight. When Ralph joined our household, he was free to wander, but he always chose to sleep in bed with us every night. The real problem was his restlessness. When Ralph was bored or not yet tired, he looked for mischief, like jumping on my dresser to see what new items he could paw onto the floor, always looking back to see if I was watching. If I ignored him, his behavior became worse.

One of the first items that drew his attention was a ceramic vase that held six wooden tulips from Amsterdam. As he slowly nudged the vase to the end of the dresser, I leaped out of bed and securely taped the vase to the top of the dresser with green painter's tape. Ralph then decided to extract those wooden tulips, flicking them off the dresser, one stem at a time. He next went after every other item until the dresser was completely cleared off. Satisfied with his work, his curiosity took him to a much more dangerous place.

Directly behind the large dresser was a narrow four-inch space that allowed access to the electrical plugs and outlets. I never imagined that this gap would present any real danger, but it was just wide enough for a cat to slip down, and too narrow to squirm back out. And sure enough, I watched in disbelief as he attempted to investigate by sticking his head and front paws into the abyss. With each movement, he slid farther down, as though trapped in quicksand, with no leverage to push himself back up.

Similar to the time he slipped behind my desk, I had to gently grip his hindquarters while slipping my other arm down under his head and belly to ease him up and out. Without my assistance, he would have been hopelessly trapped behind the 80-pound dresser.

Once he was freed, I went directly to my basement workshop and cut a piece of plywood to fit over the top of the dresser, with four additional inches of width to cover the gap to the back wall. With the gaps along the sides of the dresser still exposed, I trimmed two foam noodles to plug those spaces. Now the bedroom was "Ralph-proofed," or so I presumed.

Ralph then set his sights on my nightstand next to the bed. The smaller items on top were much more fun to slap off: travel alarm clock, eye drop dispenser, reading glasses, paperback books, pens, paper, watch, and my old flip-phone. When it was time for "lights out," we had our first reprieve, and the atmosphere changed for the better.

Ralph typically jumped up on the foot of the bed and walked up the middle, between us, in a manner we referred to as "coming up the runway." As he neared our heads, he always veered to Renee's side, then plopped down on her pillow and tucked his head under her chin. With a warm smile on her face, Renee would pull the sheet up over his body as he had this enviable ability to fall asleep within seconds.

Admittedly, it was an adorable scene—Renee and Ralph asleep together, with her arm around him... until 3 a.m. when Ralph's internal alarm clock went off. It was time for him to get up and start the "tap, tap, tap" of his soft paw on my arm, while I sensed his face only inches from my mine. I didn't dare move because I knew he was staring at me in the darkness and waiting to get my attention. Then again, "Tap, tap, tap." There was no escape.

I eventually had no other choice. Sitting up in bed, I would turn to him and say, "Ralph... do you want foooood?... foooood?" Our old window blinds allowed just enough city light to see the outline of his perky ears rotating with excitement. He may not have known the words, but he certainly understood the tone of my voice.

After I slid off the side of the bed without turning on the lamp, I would suddenly sprint into the hallway and run down the carpeted stairs with Ralph galloping right behind me. Halfway down is a landing with a window facing the back yard. At this point, I would turn 180 degrees and continue running down the last few stairs to the first-floor hallway, making another turn toward the kitchen. His bowl was always half full, but he felt it necessary to have it topped off in the middle of the night. Just another scoop of kibble, that was all he wanted.

Although Ralph still preferred to fall asleep nestled securely under Renee's chin, he always chose to wake *me* up for more food. I liked to think of it as a type of bonding between man and cat, until a near accident almost ended my life.

During what would be my final race with him in the dark, he tried passing me on the stairs, crossing over from left to right, bumping into my legs and sending me flying over the last three stairs to the mid-level landing. With such momentum, I hit the wall so hard that I thought I broke my wrists. Fortunately, I just missed putting both arms and my body through the window by mere inches. If I had hit the window and broken through the glass, the 14-foot plunge to the brick walkway below would have been deadly.

Dazed and disoriented, I slowly walked the rest of the way downstairs, noticing Ralph's silhouette, illuminated by night-light, as he waited patiently by his food bowl. Meanwhile, Renee never stirred, thanks to her earplugs.

The next morning, after I recounted the whole story to Renee, she was not sympathetic. She had repeatedly warned me about running down the stairs in the dark, reminding me that I was already accident prone. I then challenged her to take over the late-night feedings and badly miscalculated. It was like telling a child that she could not leave the dinner table until she ate three more scoops of ice cream.

But Ralph did not understand this new arrangement. While he continued his routine of snuggling with Renee at bedtime, he still chose to wake *me* up in the dead of night. The only difference now was that I would turn and *gently* tap Renee, always aware of that old adage, "Don't poke the bear."

Renee now had to get up and feed Ralph at night, except our methods were quite different. While I used to run down the stairs with Ralph, she preferred to scoop him up in her arms and carry him down, and she seldom complained. Yet Ralph was still waking me up and choosing his old technique of "tap, tap, tapping" on my forehead, but I remained completely still, not even a facial twitch.

Getting no response, he started lightly "nipping" my ears and cheeks, then gently scraping his canine tooth across the top of my bald head. Constantly being bothered and unable to get back to sleep, I could not stand it anymore. I whispered, "Reneeeeee..." No answer. I forgot about her earplugs, so I switched from "tap, tap, tapping" her, to "poke, poke, poking" her. Without saying a word, she would slip out of bed and carry Ralph downstairs while I fell back asleep. But I knew that he was not going to let me off the hook that easily.

A few weeks later, I woke up around 4 a.m. with breathing problems. I was not in any pain, but definitely concerned because of my past issues with atrial fibrillation, a condition in which the heart's electrical rhythms sometime become very irregular. As I lay awake in bed, I mentally processed my health checklist. My heart was beating steadily, no irregular heartbeats, and no pain in my chest or legs. Then I reached over and turned on the bedside lamp.

Ralph had been sitting silently in the dark on my CPAP machine, directly on top of the on/off button, and he had obviously turned it "off." No wonder I was having trouble breathing.

CPAP—which is short for "Continuous Positive Airway Pressure"—is a small medical, at-home machine to treat sleep apnea. This device is about the size of a tissue box and requires a six-foot hose that is attached to a mask or nasal buds. It provides a continuous flow of air to prevent repeated starts and stops in one's breathing during the night. Millions of people use them, and some machines tend to be a bit noisy—another reason Renee wore earplugs. Although I was a veteran CPAP user, this was new technology for Ralph and something he wasted no time investigating.

He also began a pattern of biting on my mask, slowly at first, and then becoming more aggressive, the way a dog chews on a rubber bone. My only solution was to cover my face and mask with the bedsheet and try to fall back asleep. That was nearly impossible, leaving me with only one choice.

"Reneeeeee..." Once again, I forgot about her earplugs, but

she would eventually get out of bed, as long as it was related to Ralph. His nighttime escapades seldom bothered her. Unfortunately, Ralph quickly figured out that sitting on my CPAP machine would definitely get my attention. After he turned it off one night for the third time, I jumped out of bed, turned on the lamp, and tried to wake Renee, which was difficult. In addition to the earplugs, she wore a sleep mask.

Her only comment: "He looks so cute sitting there." Then she lifted him off my machine and took him downstairs for kibble and treats. When I woke up in the morning, Ralph was tucked comfortably under her chin, the two of them snoring in varying octaves. I took a photo of them and then went down to my workshop to build a protective cover for the CPAP machine.

Using a medium-sized box, I made appropriate cutouts for the hose and electrical cord, and then inserted carefully trimmed pieces of 3/4-inch styrofoam inside the box to dampen the noise. I also drilled dozens of quarter-inch holes in the top and sides to allow air to flow into the machine. A small cat-proof flap in the front allowed me to reach inside to turn the machine on and off.

I was proud of my ingenuity and problem-solving abilities, and was looking forward to a good night's sleep. That prospect lasted for only three days.

That same week, I woke up one night to the unsettling hiss of air, similar to a tea kettle. As I lay there in the dark trying to triangulate the location of the sound, I turned on the light and noticed that Renee had her arm around Ralph. They were both sound asleep. I soon sensed the disturbance was near the CPAP machine, and a visual inspection confirmed lots of tiny holes in the six-foot plastic hose. My immediate thought—Ralph!

The hissing noise was so distracting, like fingernails on a chalk board. I got out of bed, went down to my workshop, and fetched a roll of electrical tape. Back upstairs, I wrapped the tape tightly over the holes. Ralph got up to watch. Once the lights were out, I barely closed my eyes when I heard that hissing noise again. Obviously, I missed covering some of the holes because there were so many. Renee never woke up that night, asking me in the morning why I was so crabby. I showed her the hose riddled with dozens of tiny holes, all matching Ralph's teeth.

His new obsession with the CPAP hose continued, including slapping and biting it, until one night I woke up again to that awful hissing noise. Turning on the light, I happened to look down at the side of the bed. Ralph had been sitting on the floor, in the dark, biting holes in the plastic hose as fast as a conductor punches tickets on a New York commuter train. Even after I caught him, he did not stop. I was getting desperate.

Following hours of internet research, I stumbled upon a link to several companies that sold six-foot-long fabric coverings designed to be slipped over CPAP hoses. I was so overjoyed that I ordered four, and they worked exceptionally well. Ralph immediately stopped chewing on the hoses; he did not like the taste of fleece. What a satisfying experience to outsmart a smarty cat.

With each problem I solved, another always appeared, such as when Ralph nearly fell behind my bedside nightstand. As with the dresser, there is a space for the electrical cords and outlets, leaving a narrow drop-zone into a cord-filled abyss from which no cat would be able to retreat. The solution was to trim a large pine board to fit perfectly on top of the night-stand, covering all the gaps between the corner walls and the bed.

When I stood in the middle of the bedroom and looked at our bed, each side had identical nightstands and identical lamps. Renee's side looked so neat and tidy: a corded alarm clock, her lamp, earplugs, several books, eye drops, cell phone, and a plush animal from her childhood. Ralph never disturbed her items, only mine. My side looked like it belonged to Jed Clampett of the *Beverly Hillbillies*. Rolls of toilet paper, paper towels, an old pillow, and a bath towel were stuffed tightly on the sides of my nightstand, which was topped off by an unsightly cardboard box covering the CPAP machine. It was not a pretty sight. Fortunately, our bedroom was always off-limits to all visitors.

NINE

Mouse in the house

ONE EVENING AFTER midnight, Renee and I had been reading in bed, and Ralph was already asleep on her pillow. About a minute after we turned out the lights, they were back on again. Renee and I were both sitting up in bed, each accusing the other of passing "really nasty gas." Suddenly, we looked down at Ralph, stretched out on his back in a deep slumber, oblivious to the world.

Renee jumped out of bed and went directly to the bathroom to fetch a pair of safety scissors. After lifting Ralph up off the pillow, I wrapped my arms around him, similar to securing a cow in a milking stanchion. Renee then performed a quick *snip* on his rear end, and we went back to sleep. The offensive culprit was just a small smelly "dingle-berry" stuck to his furry butt, although Renee still insisted that such unpleasant odors usually came from me.

SHARING OUR QUEEN-SIZED bed had become a bit *complicated*. When Renee started complaining about being crowded out of her space, we measured. Apparently, I occupied 40% of the bed, Ralph claimed 40%, and Renee had to make do with only 20%. In an attempt to equal things out, I moved closer to the edge, Ralph took over the extra space, and Renee gained nothing. Fortunately, she adapted well.

LOOKING BACK ON Ralph's first summer with us, he started exhibiting some unusual behavior. Whenever he and Renee were alone together, he joined her on the couch and lay tightly beside her with his head or paw always touching her. These were not one-time events; they occurred all the time, especially at night before bedtime. Even more unusual, he would often tap Renee on the arm to get her attention and then stare up into her eyes as though he wanted to tell her something. Renee said she felt like he was trying to communicate with her.

It was obvious that Ralph had imprinted on Renee, and they were becoming inseparable. Renee started referring to him as her "care cat," and I found myself becoming a bit jealous, until something strange happened. Following surgery on my nose to improve my breathing, I had to sleep for several nights sitting upright on the couch, surrounded by pillows for support. After Renee turned out the lights, I woke up 30 minutes later and found Ralph sleeping on my lap. He remained with me all night and again the following night.

I was absolutely astounded because Ralph always shared Renee's pillow every night. And he was not a lap cat, preferring to snug *next* to people, but never on their laps. For some cosmic reason, or "feline magic" as Renee called it, Ralph sensed that I was not feeling well and did his best to comfort me in his own way. Once I recovered, he never sat on my lap again, until after my rotator cuff surgery... seven years later.

At night during the summer, we could not open the bedroom windows to enjoy a cool breeze because Ralph liked to run full-speed and jump onto the windowsills. We were concerned that he was going to plow through the flimsy screens and plunge 18 feet to his demise on the concrete driveway below.

Although there is no "pet safety" aisle at Home Depot, I did find a pair of adjustable, two-part screens that slid apart to fit most windows. I placed them inside against our existing screens, providing a double buffer for extra safety. Ralph could now run and jump as fast and as forcefully as he wanted with little chance of bursting through both screens. He simply bounced off, ending our worries about scraping him off the driveway.

Another problem soon arose in our bedroom. Late one night while we were asleep, Ralph stirred and woke me up. We both heard a nearly inaudible scratching sound in the wall. I thought it might be a mouse. Ralph was more certain. He jumped onto the floor and low-crawled across the room to the return air vent. I decided to go back to sleep, leaving him to patrol the room until after sunrise.

First thing in the morning, I rummaged through the basement and found some old mousetraps. I just had to be extremely careful where I placed them—the thought of a trap snapping on Ralph's delicate paws or face was unnerving. For that reason, the only safe place for mouse-catching was inside the plumbing access in the stairwell going up to the second floor. The 16" x 20" hole in the wall was a prime spot, discreetly covered by a large framed photograph.

My preferred bait was a jar of very old peanut butter stored in the back of our pantry. I never forgot the time a visitor made himself a peanut butter sandwich without first asking. As he was spitting it into the garbage, I explained that the jar was six years old, definitely rancid, and only used as mouse bait. Following that incident, I labeled the jar with a skull and crossbones.

After removing the photograph covering the plumbing access, I bent down to pick up a handful of mousetraps. When I looked up, I was surprised to see Ralph calmly sitting *inside* the space, watching me.

"Reneeeeee... come and get your cat before he gets *trapped*."

She hastened up the stairs, scooped him out of the opening in the wall, and carried him down to the TV room. Once I had all the traps set and in position, she released him. Now it was only a matter of time.

Late that same night, Ralph and I woke up together after we both heard a "snap." I smiled and went back to sleep, while Ralph left the room to investigate. As for Renee, she never budged, thanks to her earplugs and sleep mask.

The following day, I almost forgot about the traps until I noticed Ralph sitting on the landing, staring intently at the framed photograph. I knew he was not admiring the rice fields of Southeast Asia. He was more concerned about what was *behind* the photograph. While Renee coaxed him into the TV room and closed the door, I removed the photograph and peeked inside the access hole. I was expecting one mouse... not four. This set a new record that came with a significant downside. We now had a much bigger problem than I had anticipated.

While I was delicately bagging bodies and resetting traps, Ralph was pounding on the TV room door and begging to get out so he could watch. After I shouted to Renee, "All clear, release the boy," Ralph bolted out and raced up the six carpeted stairs to the landing. There was nothing for him to see, but he certainly had a great memory.

As the weather got colder in November, the mice were beginning their indoor winter migration through the tiniest of holes in our old stone foundation. By Thanksgiving, I had already trapped 17 mice, and I told Renee that I felt like a pre-colonial French fur trapper. Renee suggested not bragging to people, adding that this was not a reason to be proud.

The following year, we set another record. I trapped 19 mice, and Ralph caught his first. He did not get to keep it. I pulled the squirmy thing from his mouth and humanely disposed of it, and Renee rewarded our little hunter with tuna treats.

At the end of winter, Renee and I had some serious discussions to figure out why we were seeing such an infestation of mice. Our neighbor suggested it was probably due to the enormous amount of bird seed that we were loading into our large-capacity bird feeders. Such an abundance of seed was attracting a lot more than birds.

We also discovered that birds are sloppy eaters. For every seed the birds ate, their beaks flicked several more onto the ground, offering an excellent buffet for our expanding mouse population. This was quite a dilemma. If we scaled back on bird food, we would attract fewer birds, leading to less excitement for Ralph, who enjoyed spending hours on his window perch watching his feathery friends. Renee voted to keep feeding the birds and suggested that I spend more time in the basement mixing cement and plugging holes in the stone foundation.

After hearing our stories, friends suggested other options such as using poison and placing traps outside. We insisted, "No way." Various poisons and snap-traps could be extremely harmful to Ralph's outdoor cat friends, Earl Gray and Mikki, and to a whole host of other small mammals and birds.

Adding to my concerns, I woke up one morning after hearing a disturbing new sound in the ceiling directly above the bed. As it grew louder, Renee also woke up. We were both startled and confused, especially since the noise was much too loud to be rodents. Then we realized the commotion was coming from outside—"plop, plop, plop, plop"—as if dozens of scuba divers with large flippers were walking on our steep roof.

I rushed downstairs. Ralph was already on his perch, his face pressed up against the window, tail wagging nonstop. What a scene. Directly below our bird feeders was a flock of 45 ducks, quacking wildly and trampling the snow as they foraged for seeds that the birds had knocked from the feeders a day earlier. It was not uncommon to see a few mallards in our yard, but this many was highly unusual. Several neighbors recounted watching these flocks flying in circles and landing on our house, forming a single-file line across the peak of our roof. Once the ducks were in position, they marched down the roof together, hence all the noise.

While ducks are graceful gliders during water landings, they are not suited for parachuting off a 20-foot roof. Despite flapping their wings to break their fall, the lucky ones crash-landed in the soft snow, while the less fortunate bounced off the concrete driveway with quite a thud.

As the feeding frenzy continued daily for several weeks, Ralph enjoyed all the excitement. I also enjoyed it, until I saw the snow in our back yard covered with blackish excrement, like too many fudge sprinkles on vanilla ice cream. It was a small price to pay for living in "The Mild Kingdom."

After many months of sleeping with us and getting up only once per night, Ralph suddenly decided he needed to wake up every 30 to 45 minutes, beginning at 3 a.m., and it was not for more food. He just kept tapping one of us on the head or arm with his right paw. If we ignored him, he picked up the pace using both front paws like a feather-weight boxer, "Pow, pow, pow."

This led Renee and me to suffer from sleep deprivation, and we concluded that there was only one practical solution. We needed to close the bedroom door at night. During our first attempt, we placed Ralph on his window perch and then rushed upstairs, closing the bedroom door behind us. As we were reading in bed, we could hear him outside in the hallway.

First came the "tap, tap, tap" on the door with his soft

paws, interspersed with "meows" every 30 seconds. And he would not stop. During his second act, he composed an aria of heart-wrenching "meows." I felt we had no choice; we had to ignore him. But after fifteen minutes of sad songs, with no intermission, we surrendered. I got up and opened the door. Ralph immediately ran inside, jumped up on the bed, and snuggled under Renee's chin. Such a cute sight. Surely, he had learned a valuable lesson.

Two hours later, "tap, tap, tap." Then again, "tap, tap, tap."

"Reneeeeee. What are we going to do with him?" Without replying, she tossed aside her covers, scooped him up in her arms, and carried him downstairs, not bothering to turn on the lights. I admired her navigational skills in total darkness.

After all this turmoil and for unknown reasons, Ralph abruptly stopped waking me up. Instead, he focused all his attentions on Renee. Four or five times each night, he would tap her face and neck, and lightly nip her face. And then came the licking. Renee said the first lick on her cheek was actually cute, a "love kiss" as she called it. The second lick was still OK, but as more licks followed, they became painful. Ralph's tongue was the equivalent of 60-grit sandpaper.

To avoid these painful, exfoliating licks on her exposed skin, Renee started pulling the sheet over her head, only to encounter the "paw, paw, paw" from his little paws. There seemed to be no relief, until Renee fled from the bedroom. Two or three times a week, she took her pillow and a blanket, and went downstairs to sleep on the couch. Surprisingly, Ralph followed her down and slept peacefully with her for the rest of the night, which was another of those cat phenomena that I would never understand.

Within a month, his nighttime licking subsided to what Renee termed as "manageable levels," but Ralph was still waking her up far too often. And then he started waking me up again. After consulting a number of friends for possible solutions, there was a general consensus—"Close your bedroom door at night." Although we had already tried that once, we decided to try again, unaware that we were descending to the sixth level of Dante's Inferno.

That night, Renee hugged and kissed Ralph before setting him adrift in the hallway, like the abandonment of Moses along the Nile. After closing our bedroom door, she was sad and weepy for not having her furry orange friend nestling under her chin. Ralph must have felt the same way because he began banging on the door, accompanied by a range of sad, pitiful "meows," imploring us to let him into the bedroom. Renee and I remained steadfast. She inserted her earplugs, while I put a pillow over my head. I called it "tough love."

Ralph continued pounding on the door; his meows were relentless. Without a better solution, we'd never get any sleep. It was already past midnight when I got out of bed and started planning a defensive barrier, similar to the Maginot Line, a series of fortifications that the French had built to protect them from the German army prior to WWII, except the Germans advanced around it. Unlike the French, my fortifications could not be circumvented.

To create a diversion, Renee escorted Ralph down to the kitchen, topping off his bowl of kibble and rushing back upstairs. With our bedroom door opened only ten inches, I slipped two extra-large sofa cushions out into the hallway, leaning them against the door. I also squeezed six pillows through the opening, piling them on top, with a blanket thrown over everything for good measure. Then I carefully closed the door.

My cushiony mountain in the hallway stood almost six feet tall, creating a barrier that no cat could penetrate. I was proud of my ingenuity, until Renee smiled and shook her head. "So, what happens when I have to get up and go to the bathroom in the middle of the night?"

I turned off the lights and hoped that our bladders would hold out until morning. On a positive note, we now had the whole bed to ourselves, but before I could fall asleep, I heard a muffled "mau." A minute later another "mau." These were sad, one-syllable calls for attention, the ones that pull on your heart-strings. I had to keep reminding myself, "Love with limits."

Soon more soft and muted sounds drifted through the door. "Mau... mau... mau." I ignored Ralph; he needed to learn to sleep alone. Minutes later, the next wave hit, now even sadder, followed by silence. In that moment, I could sense that Sir Ralph Edmund Hillary was in the process of scaling his pillowy Mt. Everest. Managing to reach the summit, he started banging on the top of the door, followed by a series of lengthy "meows."

I nudged Renee several times. She mumbled that she heard nothing, perhaps because of her earplugs. After another ten minutes lying in the dark, I could not stand it anymore. Ralph sounded like he was dying in the hallway, so I turned on the light and woke Renee. She said, "Fine, let him in."

It was already past 1:00 a.m. when I opened the bedroom door and was met by an avalanche of cushions and pillows cascading into the bedroom. A moment later, Ralph casually walked over them, jumped into the bed, and snuggled under

Renee's chin. She was smiling, Ralph was purring, and I was wide awake. At some point in the middle of the night, I tripped over those pillows on my way to the bathroom. I had forgotten they were still scattered in the doorway. My Maginot Line had failed. Never again would we close our bedroom door at night.

It took nearly two years to finally settle into a mutually agreeable sleep routine. We were all going to bed much later now, the three of us snugged together with Ralph always in the middle. Renee was still OK getting up in the middle of the night to carry Ralph downstairs and replenish his bowl of kibble, as long as it was just once per night.

With the passing of time, I actually found myself becoming quite attached to Ralph, despite all his bad behaviors. Having a feline in our cozy home started to make sense. I even believed that our lives were back to being wonderful again, until the following fall when the mice returned, and this time it would be an invasion.

TEN

The Trojan cat

ON A MONDAY morning in 2012, the New York Stock Exchange was set to open in exactly two minutes. I was preparing to buy shares of Starbucks stock in my IRA account. At that moment, Ralph jumped up on my desk and plopped down next to my laptop, and gradually inched closer to the keyboard.

With Ralph so close, I was forced to type the order with my left forefinger—symbol: "SBUX," action: "Buy," quantity: "200 shares." Meanwhile, my right arm was fully extended, going up and down like a short-circuited railroad crossing-gate to separate Ralph from the keyboard. He tried going over and then under my arm, all the while I was shouting to Renee for help. As she rushed in and scooped him off the desk, I pressed the key to place my order, only to receive an error message: "This order exceeds your buying power," financial jargon for saying I did not have enough money.

Totally perplexed, even fearing that my IRA account had

been hacked, I quickly scrolled through my records, checked my balances, and reviewed my original order. I finally realized that I didn't make a mistake. But Ralph certainly did. He had managed to stretch his paw just far enough to tap and hold the "9" key as I was entering the quantity. Instead of 200 shares of Starbucks stock, my order indicated a desired purchase of 2,009,999 shares, which would have cost over $110 million.

After that experience, Ralph was "banned for life" from being near my desk during trading hours. If he was serious about buying stock, he should have waited a few more years to buy shares of a new company called Chewy.com.

AT SOME POINT in the middle of the night, I sprang up in bed, certain there was another woman in our bedroom. I reached over, turned on the bedside lamp, and was surprised to see Ralph sitting on my iPhone. He had somehow activated Siri who repeated, "Sorry, I did not understand."

I laughed as I pleaded with Siri, "Please tell my cat to go to sleep." Siri was unable to help, but all the commotion woke Renee. She slipped out of bed and carried Ralph downstairs, and suggested that I put my phone on *silent mode* at night. But that proved to be such a hassle because I typically forgot to switch it back on in the morning. My solution came years later when Apple's newest iPhones added a fingerprint ID feature that would not recognize a paw print. That was incentive enough to upgrade to a new phone… all thanks to Ralph, who should have received a commission.

THE CONCEPT OF cat trees was new to me. Renee explained that cats enjoy climbing and being high off the floor, offering them a safe, secure, and comfortable spot to observe their surroundings or simply to relax. Fortunately, there was no need for us to buy one because I chose to build one myself.

After purchasing a six-foot 4x4 for the center post, I screwed it to an 18-inch round pine base and attached two steps and a roomy platform on the top, which I covered with plush carpeting. The result was a masterpiece. I placed it by the dining-room window where it remained unwanted and unused. Ralph showed no interest. Instead, he preferred his padded window perch only two feet away.

A few days later, I moved the cat tree to the TV room. Ralph was curious enough to jump up on it twice, then quickly found it boring, choosing instead to lie next to us on the couch. I was not that upset because the first step of his cat tree now doubled as a convenient end table for our beverages and snacks. The downside was that it blocked access to the closet.

After a month of non-use, Ralph's custom-made $80 cat tree was relocated to the garage and eventually gifted to Peaches, my nephew's cat. She appreciated it very much, unlike our ungrateful Ralph.

I OFTEN WONDERED how people dealt with bad behavior from their own pets, especially after Ralph turned out to be such a disruptor—trashing my desk, disabling cables and electronics, knocking over flower vases and potted plants, trying to rip through the window blinds, and waking us at all hours.

For all his bad behavior, I had yet to figure out an appropriate punishment. Take away his toys? Remove the gravy from his wet food? No more tuna treats? Get a large intimidating dog? Perhaps confine him for an hour to a room without a window perch?

However, none of Ralph's antics ever bothered Renee. She took them all in stride. Her love of cats superseded any personal annoyance or damage to our house or possessions. She also knew that I was joking about punishing Ralph. When I overdid the cat humor, she pushed back and pretended to call the ASPCA. Meanwhile, I continued to insist that a porcelain cat would have looked very nice on the bookshelf and would have spared us all the problems of having a real one.

During the daytime, our second-floor bedroom was perhaps the most peaceful part of the house, only because Ralph avoided it until bedtime. However, the other rooms on that floor—the double-sized bathroom, the walk-in closet, and the huge storeroom—provided wonderful play areas, but also posed many problems for Ralph's safety and for my sanity.

Having grown up with only one bathroom to share with

my seven siblings and our parents, I purposefully designed and built a spacious bathroom with double sinks and a walk-in shower. Tucked in the corner is a separate bathtub sunk into a surrounding tiled platform. This offers a perfect area for Renee to display her impressive collection of large scallop and clam shells, all lined up neatly against the walls around the tub.

The bathroom's south-facing windows and skylight give the room a terrarium atmosphere, ideal for our assortment of plants, including an enormous spider plant that Ralph found insatiably delicious. Without supervision, this bathroom was permanently "off limits" to Ralph, and not just because he once jumped into the toilet or knocked over and broke four flowerpots.

Whenever Renee or I were upstairs in the bathroom, Ralph would appear and gently start pawing on the door. If it did not open, he would start pounding on it. He absolutely hated being closed out of any room if he knew one of us was inside.

I once accidentally left the door slightly ajar while I was showering. Ralph slipped inside and made a stealthy run to the bathtub. Even with the shower running, I could hear the seashells crashing down as Ralph ran around the tub's platform knocking them over, one after another, like he was inside a pinball machine.

I was dripping wet and could only do one thing, "Reneeeee … Reneeeeee." As she rushed into the bathroom, Ralph jumped down and ran out the door past her. After rearranging her shell collection, she scolded me for not securing the door. No mention of Ralph's bad behavior.

Admittedly, it was funny when Renee and I would both be brushing our teeth and watching Ralph in the mirror as he slinked through the partially open door and lay down quietly on the floor behind us. If he felt he was undetected, he would do a slow crawl toward the baby spider plants that hung down on long stems from the mother plant. If we did not intervene, he would stretch upward and strip the tender shoots off the stems and swallow them within seconds.

His other approach was to attack the spider plant from atop the toilet tank, so I placed a wicker box on top as a barrier. He simply climbed on top of it and then stretched all the way to the windowsill, only to have the box slide off in the other direction, sending him plummeting toward the floor.

Fortunately, I was nearby and caught Ralph as he started to fall. That was terrifying because the pointed end of the toilet-cleaning brush was facing upward in its holder, directly below where he would have impaled himself. Even Renee was alarmed at this close call, so the toilet brush was immediately relocated safely behind the toilet tank. Oblivious to such hazards, Ralph maintained his ravenous appetite for our tender houseplants, and when left unchecked, he would munch away like a baby brontosaurus. That led to other potential and serious dangers that had to be considered.

As our poison-control expert, Renee regularly researched which flowers and plants we could keep indoors and which had to remain outside in our garden. Her many varieties of lilies were beautiful, but also toxic to cats. Luckily, our giant spider plant was nontoxic, but we discovered that cats are often drawn to spider plants for their mildly hallucinogenic properties, affecting cats, not humans. As for catnip, Ralph had no interest, and he was not alone. It is estimated that 50% of all cats exhibit no reaction at all to catnip.

Aside from all our plants, we also had other safety concerns in our bathroom. The six-foot-long vanity offered the most *goodies*: toothbrushes, toothpaste, razors, ointments, cosmetics, tubes of creams, jars of lotions, and prescription pills, even though they had cat-proof tops. I once dropped a blood pressure pill on the floor and Ralph rushed for it immediately. If I had not instinctively grabbed him by the scruff of his neck, our next stop would have been the veterinary E.R.

Another area of concern was the ten-foot walk-in closet with clothes racks and shelving on both walls. Although the wide opening and angled ceiling did not allow for a door, Renee and I loved the easy access. So did Ralph. The blouses, dresses, pants, and shirts—all on hangers—were like magnets attracting the long hair that Ralph shed on a daily basis. It was often difficult for me to find a pair of black pants that wasn't coated with cat hair. Worse yet, the dry cleaner refused to take the orange hair off my pants, explaining that I had to remove it *before* I brought them in for dry cleaning

That made for quite a dilemma. With no door on the walk-in closet, I had to figure out a way to keep Ralph out. Down in my workshop, I cut a sheet of cardboard into a 30" by 40" piece and glued strips of duct tape on top, adhesive-side up, creating a homemade "sticky board." While Renee and Ralph were watching TV, I went back upstairs and laid the tacky cardboard on the floor in front of the opening to the closet. When Renee saw it, she was not impressed, saying it looked terrible. I agreed. Duct tape has never been known as an attractive product, but I didn't care, so long as it kept Ralph out of the closet.

Then Renee made another observation, "How am I going

to get in and out of the closet? Do I have to jump over it each time?" My suggestion was that we treat it like a drawbridge, lifting it up each time we walked in or out of the closet. Renee used the word "ridiculous" and also thought it would be cruel if Ralph got stuck on it like a bug on flypaper.

In the midst of this discussion, Ralph slipped past us and took his first step on the board's tacky surface, and then stepped back to check his paw for residue. Pacing back and forth, he studied the board with curiosity. I turned to Renee with a grin of success, while she looked down at Ralph and then smiled back at me. In a burst of speed, Ralph dashed across the board and back again and was now sitting at Renee's feet. So smug, the both of them.

Without saying a word, I retreated to the basement and cobbled together a second sticky board, laying it behind the first one. Ralph simply ran across them both with his teflon-like paws. This was a complete waste of an afternoon. I picked up both boards, folded them in half, and deposited them in the trash.

A few days later, while searching the internet for another solution, I discovered plastic spike mats for pets. These were advertised as safe and humane, reminding me of the much larger spike mats that police use to stop speeding cars during a chase. I ordered two—the ones for pets, not cars. Upon delivery, I immediately took them upstairs and carefully positioned them on the closet floor. Renee was upset, not just for Ralph's sake, but also concerned that some morning she might step on them with her bare feet.

Apparently, that would not be an issue for Ralph. I noticed that he was already lying down on the first spike mat, while intently watching me position the second one. As I was shaking my head in disbelief, he got up and casually walked across the other spike mat. This had been a complete waste of time and money, and as I turned to pick them up, the heel of my bare foot made contact with the first mat. That was definitely painful! Without hesitation, I threw those mats into the trash.

Throughout my entire professional career, I was regarded for my problem-solving abilities and my perseverance, and retirement did not change that. I kept searching until I found one last option—a battery-powered shock mat that was activated when stepped on.

I was certain that a tiny jolt of low-voltage current on his soft, tender paws would be a great deterrent. But once again, Renee did not like my idea and said it sounded downright cruel. She also reminded me that she walks into that closet several times a day, so was I planning to shock her, too?

I assured her that retailers wouldn't sell anything that would be harmful to pets. She was skeptical and promised that if I made such a purchase, she would first test it out on my face. Before placing the order, I called my friend Tom to ask if he knew about these shock mats. Not only had he heard about them, he had purchased a pair to keep his own two cats off his desk.

"So, what did you think of them?" I asked.

Tom started laughing, then offered to give me his two mats, explaining they were "useless." His smart felines simply jumped over them or navigated around them. I waved the white flag. Ralph won again. The closet was his to destroy. But after all of my anxiety and concern, Ralph seldom went into the walk-in closet again. He apparently had too many other fun and intriguing options.

The last area of concern on the second floor was the store-room adjacent to the walk-in closet. This 280-square-foot space is ideal for storing off-season clothing, suitcases, books, overflow kitchen gadgets, memorabilia, old files, extra furni-ture, and bulk purchases of nonperishable products. We ini-tially allowed Ralph to follow us inside the storeroom, until he started enjoying it too much and did not want to come out.

With a vast amount of tightly packed items piled to the ceiling, we soon realized that the storeroom is a dangerous place for a cat. The storage racks are heavy-duty plastic, but all the shelves are honeycombed with large holes, big enough for a cat's foot to easily slip through, and that is exactly what happened.

On one occasion when Ralph jumped up to a narrow space between two boxes, both of his front legs disappeared through the shelf holes and were dangling out the underside. He was stunned and stuck. If he had fallen sideways off the edge, he could have easily sprained or broken one or both of his front legs. He was lucky that I was there to lift him out. After another similar incident, I declared that Ralph was per-manently banned from the storeroom but, then again, many of our rooms had already become "off limits."

Renee suggested I should relax, saying, "Ralph is just be-ing a curious cat." But he still had to stay out of the storeroom, which was a challenge for us. He soon devised a new tech-nique, positioning himself quietly against the wall behind the shoe rack and waiting patiently for me to open the storeroom door. And then "whoosh." He would bolt inside and disappear deep into the abyss to explore and hide.

I was convinced that if Ralph had been on the side of the Trojans 3,200 years ago, they could have used him, instead of a wooden horse, to sneak into the city of Troy.

On another occasion as I was exiting the storeroom, I caught a brief glimpse of an orange tail slipping past me. I immediately called out, "Reneeeeee... I need your help," and I really did. Once Ralph managed to get inside, it required a team effort to get him out. He would remain silent and still, as Renee and I crawled around on our hands and knees, searching among four-foot deep shelves.

Finding him was only the first step. Coaxing him to come out was much more difficult. Tuna treats did not work, despite my pretending to eat them. This generally turned into a standoff—we on our stomachs, while he remained far back in the shadows. One solution was to start unloading the shelves, but that proved fruitless. Once we got close to him, he would slink to the next aisle, forcing us to put all the boxes back in place before trying again.

During one unsuccessful extraction, we simply gave up, turned off the light, and closed the door. The windowless room became pitch black, like deep space. Small children would have been terrified. Not Ralph. Ten minutes later we opened the door, allowing him to exit at will, but he waited another half hour before he finally came out after realizing it was no fun to play alone.

On those occasions when Ralph became obstinate about not coming out, Renee intervened. She is remarkably flexible from her childhood ballet days and would have made a great spelunker. Flat on her belly, she would crawl under and between the shelves, moving aside small boxes as though they were rocks in a cave blocking her path. Ralph had met his match. When they were face to face, she would extend her arms and offer him comforting words as they both squirmed back out together. That was amazing. I never could have done that.

Renee noted that the real problem with the storeroom was not Ralph, but rather the *person* who failed to completely close the door after entering or leaving the room. Forced to admit that I was the biggest offender, I sincerely promised that I would never again be so careless.

Several months later, while pretending to be asleep on his window perch, Ralph heard the storeroom door open and raced upstairs, slipping past me again. It took two hours to coax him out. Renee was away at the time, so I never mentioned it. Any incident involving just Ralph and *me* was best left untold.

ELEVEN

First floor mayhem

DURING THE MIDDLE of the night, I got up and went to the bathroom. No need to turn on the light since I knew the route well. After returning to bed, I heard a distinct scratching and wondered if I had baited the mouse traps. Then I heard another sound, faint and muffled, and I know that mice didn't meow.

Without turning on the light, I shuffled back to the bathroom, opened the door, and felt furry hair grazing my leg and moving past me in the direction of our bed. Ralph must have followed me into the bathroom in the dark and got shut inside. But once we were back in bed, he immediately fell asleep while I lay awake. I could still hear that darn mouse.

A COPY-PAPER BOX lid made a perfect container for Ralph's huge collection of small toys. He also had dozens of six-inch stuffed animals, including a whale, shark, seal, panda, crab, lobster, lion, penguin, octopus, seagull, caterpillar, manatee, kangaroo, koala, among other assorted animals. All were presents that we brought back from various trips in the U.S. and abroad, including a solar-powered, twirling bird from the Amsterdam flower market.

Despite being lavished with such gifts, the inexpensive toy mice were his favorites, until one day when I reached into the wastepaper basket and retrieved an empty spool from a roll of Scotch tape. Tossing it to Ralph, he used the spool as a puck to play hockey on our wooden floors, often carrying it to other rooms for an "away game." The empty spool became his favorite toy. In hindsight, we could have saved a lot of money by skipping those pricey stuffed animals and simply buying more rolls of Scotch tape.

I HAVE ALWAYS enjoyed creating homemade birthday cards for family and friends, and my hobby soon attracted Ralph's interest. He seemed drawn to arts and crafts, but mostly toward the supplies.

On one occasion, a loose piece of double-sided tape got stuck to Ralph's paw, so he used his other paw to get it off. The tape went back and forth from one paw to the other until he savagely bit it off, only to get it stuck to the side of his face. Once he managed to flick it off, he leaped on it for a final kill and again got it stuck on his paw. After allowing me to peel it off, he jumped down from my desk and left me alone.

The next time I was crafting cards, Ralph returned to help, but this time he had no interest in the double-sided tape. He would not bite it, touch it, or go near it. However, he did want access to the dozens of pens, pencils, and colored markers that he knew were inside my desk drawer. Pawing at the handle was an indication that he wanted me to open the top drawer for him.

I laughed out loud. There was no chance of opening that drawer for Ralph, not after he completely emptied all the contents twice before, with some items never being recovered. It was clear that he was more of an art thief than an artist.

Renee and I agreed that our kitchen was a danger zone where most accidents occur, such as stepping on Ralph's paws or tail, or tripping over him. He also had a tendency to slide off counters, play with knives and forks, and get shut inside the cabinets. However, our gas stove was our greatest concern, especially with boiling pots, sizzling fry pans, and a very hot oven.

During one of Ralph's culinary explorations, he got too close to the gas stove while I was boiling water in the teakettle. As soon as I noticed, I scooped him off the counter, then realized that the high flame had singed the whiskers from the left side of his face. I was relieved to see he wasn't hurt, but he did look like someone had used a curling iron on his remaining whiskers.

Then I had an even scarier thought. What would I say to Renee? I decided to keep quiet, hoping she would not notice. Besides, the whiskers would grow back in two or three months according to Google. I tried to remain calm when she returned home and scooped up Ralph to give him a big hug. Ten seconds later, she yelled, "What the heck happened to Ralph?"

I replied, "What are you talking about?" Feigning ignorance was always the safest response, but after an intense interrogation, I cracked. "Ahhhh... maybe he got too close to the stove?" I quickly walked away hoping this matter would be forgotten. It was not, and I should have kept my mouth shut because Renee later admitted that she thought Ralph's whisker problems had to do with a vitamin deficiency.

Since our galley kitchen is ten feet long with cabinets and appliances on both sides, it was perfect for the two of us, until we added a cat. Then it became a bit too crowded. While preparing meals, we always had to be aware that our furry friend was quietly lurking behind us on the floor. This was especially worrisome when moving hot pots and pans off the stove. To avoid accidents, we relied on a verbal shoutout: "Eyes on Ruffies," similar to the "mind the gap" warning on train platforms in London.

When Renee and I were elsewhere in the house, Ralph would often venture into the kitchen for no apparent reason other than to satisfy his curiosity. I once caught him standing precariously on top of our espresso machine. His body was stretched upward with his head inside the bottom shelf of a wall cabinet, the one with assorted crackers, cookies, and snacks. He wasn't at all concerned that I was looking over his right shoulder, only inches away. I didn't really care about his interest in snacks. The real mystery was how he managed to open the cabinet door.

A few days later, I found him quietly sitting on the dinner plates inside another cabinet. He apparently used a UPS package on the kitchen counter as a step-stool to stretch upward and climb inside. A more serious concern was his preference to explore the cabinet under the sink, climbing among various spray cleaners, toxic chemicals, pails, brushes, and assorted disinfectants. Most of these products are not healthy for a cat to be touching, licking, or sniffing. But once again, I couldn't imagine how he opened those cabinet doors.

More concerning was his vanishing act one evening at dinnertime when Renee repeatedly tapped a fork against his bowl, ringing the "dinner bell." After a minute of furious fork action, I was surprised the bowl did not crack. Ralph was still a "no show," which was highly unusual.

As we were about to search the house, Renee heard a metallic noise coming from an area near the stove. Narrowing the sound to the pots-and-pans cabinet, Renee opened the door and rolled out the bottom drawer. Her concern turned to laughter when she saw Ralph comfortably sitting *inside* the pasta pot. I also started laughing and promptly rolled him back inside. Renee immediately rolled the drawer back out and gently lifted the pot with Ralph still inside.

"Just put the pot on the stove," I joked, "and add some water so we can make 'orange cat soup' for dinner." But after I was scolded for my sophomoric remark, I pointed out that it wasn't me who closed Ralph inside the cabinet—I had not been in the kitchen all day. Regardless of any accusations, the kitchen cabinets had to be secured, and the local hardware store had the perfect solution: small magnetic brackets. After I attached them to the inside of the doors and rails, the magnets engaged when the doors were closed. Now the kitchen cabinets were "cat-proofed," so Ralph turned his attentions elsewhere.

"Crash." I heard that sound coming from the kitchen one morning while I was still upstairs in bed. A clay pot on the windowsill was in pieces in the sink, along with lots of dirt and a plant with exposed roots. A week later, another small flowerpot crashed into the sink, prompting a new rule: no more clay pots in the kitchen. Not long after, one of our new plastic flowerpots *mysteriously* fell into the sink, forcing us to amend the rules. Only plastic flowers in plastic pots were allowed in the kitchen window.

Meanwhile, I walked into the kitchen one afternoon and observed Ralph doing a full stretch from the edge of the countertop to the other windowsill, which is five feet off the floor and centered between the two sides of the galley kitchen. This narrow sill is only two inches wide, barely enough room for two paws, but he jumped anyway, getting himself seriously stuck and unable to move either forward or backward.

Before I could rush to his aid, he lost his balance, falling headfirst into the plastic garbage bin. Fortunately, there was plenty of trash inside to cushion his fall. He was not hurt, but he was coated with spicy arrabbiata sauce and bits of linguine. His unsuccessful balance-beam performance was tame compared to a much more dangerous stunt, during which he was preparing to leap from the top of the refrigerator to that same narrow windowsill. Just as his head was bobbing up and down, trying to judge the distance and trajectory for his jump, I intervened and lowered him to the floor, averting certain disaster.

Stopping any future attempts was easy. I simply placed five boxes of breakfast cereal on top of the refrigerator to block his access. Then I filled in the remaining open spaces with our blender, a mixing bowl, an old bottle of whiskey still in its holiday box, and four rolls of paper towels. The top of the refrigerator was now completely inaccessible, but at a cost of making our kitchen look much more cluttered. I justified it to Renee, "Safety over beauty."

Adjacent to the kitchen is the 12-foot dining room with a rectangular table and four chairs. On the outside wall, three double-hung windows facing southeast flood the room with natural light. This provided an ideal spot for an antique accessory table, repurposed with four plush bathroom carpets, one on top of the other, and two baby blankets, creating a perfect nest for Ralph to gaze out the window or nap in the sun. Getting to his window perch was easy. He went from chair to table, followed by a simple step across to his perch. So simple and so effortless, until we sat down to eat.

Trying to enjoy breakfast was always a challenge. Ralph delighted in sticking his head into my bowl or plate to examine whatever I was eating: eggs, toast, cereal, oatmeal, or fruit. But Ralph's real enjoyment took place when we invited guests over for dinner. Always wanting to be included, he'd nestle on his dining room perch and face the table so he could easily focus on our guests throughout the whole meal and act as though he was part of the conversation. Most guests found it adorable; I found it distracting.

If only one guest was dining with us, Ralph would step across from his perch and take the spot on the table where the fourth place setting would have been. One friend who did not like pets found it unsettling to have a cat staring at him while he ate. He also felt it was unsanitary, but all our other guests viewed Ralph as the evening's entertainment. Even though he could not talk, his presence was greatly enjoyed by everyone, which made me wonder if our guests were coming to see us or him.

Although our dining room is sparse on decorations, Renee always maintained a vase with flowers in the middle of the dining room table. The vase had to be sturdy and not too tall, otherwise Ralph tended to knock it over, like the one full of cattails which he could not resist biting and pawing on. Within minutes, the table was covered with water and the floor littered with broken glass. But overall, our dining room remained a relatively peaceful area, a demilitarized zone that Ralph mostly respected.

The main focal point of our house is the living room. Years earlier, I had restored the original French doors and built an intricate, solid oak fireplace mantel reminiscent of the 1920s. As wonderful as this remodeled living space turned out, it is also the least-used room in the house. For Ralph, it was more of a pass-through on his way to the front door, which leads directly onto the screened porch facing the sidewalk and the park.

Perhaps the living room lacked enough *stuff* to pique his interest, or he didn't like our new sofa—the one he pooped on during his first week in residence. However, we eventually discovered that the living room is actually a rather nice, tranquil place to hang out. With Renee away three days a week at her part-time job, Ralph and I were enjoying each other's companionship. While I sat with my iPad or a book, he napped nearby, not bothered that my feet were stretched across and resting within inches of his face. Sometimes, he even sniffed and licked my toes.

As I often paused to admire this newfound peace and tranquility between Ralph and me, I tried to fathom why I had never liked cats. I was growing quite attached to Ralph, and he actually seemed to like me, until I realized I was becoming a bit too complacent.

The second time Renee flew to New Hampshire to visit her parents, she left me home alone with Ralph for five full days, and things went downhill quickly. On the first morning, I threw out my back while bending down to scoop poop from his litter box. Then in the middle of the night, Ralph started waking me up every hour, and I was not about to carry him downstairs the way Renee always did.

On the third day, while I was sitting in the overstuffed, living room swivel chair with a heating pad on my back, Ralph calmly walked into the room and jumped up on the back of the chair, focusing his attention on the fireplace mantel. Knowing that he wanted to jump up onto the mantel, I started swiveling the chair like a merry-go-round. He held on tight; I got very dizzy. When I finally stopped, he made the leap anyway, landing on the nine-inch-wide mantel, which was elaborately decorated with all of Renee's cherished Christmas decorations.

"Ralph...get down from there!"

He knew immediately that he was in big trouble and quickly scurried from one end to the other, sweeping all of the decorations onto the floor. Garland, assorted figurines, battery-operated candles, strings of miniature lights, tiny artificial spruce trees, and framed photos, all of which Renee had recently dug out of the storeroom and positioned with great care to brighten the holidays.

Retracing his steps across the now bare mantel, Ralph leaped onto the floor and ran to his perch in the back bedroom to watch the birds, pretending everything was just fine. Hanging in the window just above his head was a bright red Christmas stocking. I doubt he understood when I said, "Don't expect to get anything in your stocking this year," which was not true. Renee had already purchased more presents for him than she had ever bought for me.

In spite of his behavior, Ralph did look cute lying on his window perch with the birds and snow-covered garden outside in the background. Such adorable scenes were often featured in our customized, annual holiday cards. As for the mess he created on the fireplace mantel, I acted like any responsible husband by picking up all the decorations and putting them in several large boxes. This was not my fault. Ralph was to blame; he caused the mess. When Renee returned home from her trip, she questioned why I had not put all the decorations back on the mantel. I tried to explain that I don't have a gift for interior design like she does, but that was a poor excuse. I should have led with my "sore back" story.

When things settled down and the holidays were behind us, Ralph and I were again enjoying our time together in the sparsely furnished living room. In addition to the couch and swivel chair, there are only two narrow side tables: one for the stereo, the other for a lamp and a vase of flowers in front of the window. As Ralph lay next to me one afternoon while I read a book, I should not have been surprised when our truce was again shattered. That nearby lamp and vase finally became too tempting.

Fortunately, the lamp is very heavy and its cord had been coated with sticky, anti-cat paste and hot pepper flakes. He knew to avoid the cord, but the vase of beautiful flowers was too tantalizing, until he discovered they were artificial.

Watching him taste the fake flowers was funny, until we made eye contact and he purposefully pushed the vase off the edge of the table onto the hardwood floor, causing an explosion of glass. That prompted our purchase of an elegant plastic vase for the fake flowers. For added safety, we filled the vase with pea gravel. Now it was unbreakable and too heavy for him to nudge off the end of the table. If he ever tried, I was prepared to glue the vase to the tabletop.

Ralph's next target was the other side table, opposite the fireplace, which held our stereo and speakers, and a half-dozen framed photos. He tried "rewiring" the tuner and speakers by pawing and gnawing on the wires, and tried to adjust the volume knob with his teeth. He quickly lost interest in music when he stepped on top of the DVD player and the lid popped open. He was so startled that he jumped off the stereo and knocked all the framed photos onto the floor. After cleaning up the broken glass, we switched to plastic frames with no glass and secured all the stereo wiring to the wall with painter's tape.

The last room on the first floor is the back "bedroom." Renee converted this room into her office, complete with a six-foot-tall bookcase filled with books, treasured mementos, artwork, and many photos of Ralph. Against the adjacent wall is her new campaign desk with barely enough room for her laptop, inkjet printer, notebooks, art supplies, and a maritime tidal clock that is of no use in Wisconsin. All her treasures should have been a magnet for any cat but, surprisingly, Ralph never disturbed any of her belongings. He enjoyed the room solely for the window, which offers an ideal view of the birds and animals in the back yard.

We initially put a TV tray in front of that window, and within months we added a second. This arrangement became known as his "double-wide." We also enhanced his perch by adding four small bathroom rugs, one on top of the other, just as we had done for his dining-room perch. And because of his obsessive bird-watching, we felt compelled to add a few more bird feeders, which meant putting up another shepherd's hook outside the back window.

Since most shepherd's hooks are mass-produced and fairly weak, a friend cut and welded three of them together into an unbendable monster that I termed a "herdsman's staff." Its triple-thick base with four hooks could easily support a combination of flower baskets and bird feeders, or one gymnast. It was so sturdy that I had a second one made the following year.

With all this capacity in so many bird feeders, we soon realized the need for much more bird food. By midsummer of Ralph's sixth year with us, our garage contained 60 cases of suet and 350 pounds of assorted birdseed that we stored in three 55-gallon, shiny new garbage cans.

Ralph and his bird friends were extremely happy... and so were the mice.

TWELVE

Let's go camping

ONE PLEASANT SUMMER afternoon as I was backing the car out of the driveway, I suddenly slammed on the brakes. Renee was gardening nearby, so I called out to her, "Hey! Come quick and look in the back seat."

Pressing her face against the car window, she started laughing. "Oh, that is *sooo* cute." Mikki, our friendly neighborhood cat, was sitting behind me in the back seat and eager to go for a ride. Apparently, while the rear hatch had been open, she jumped inside and made herself comfortable. I never noticed her, but Ralph certainly did. He was meowing, nonstop, through the screen from his window perch above the driveway. He probably wanted to join Mikki for a joy ride. Sadly for them, neither would be going anywhere together, unless they wanted to pay a social visit to the vet.

WHENEVER I BACKED the car out of the garage, I always glanced at my side mirror to look for Ralph, who typically nestled in his window perch and watched us leave. On one particular day when I didn't see him, I asked Renee, "Did you say 'goodbye' to Ralph?"

She responded, "No, did you?" Already halfway down the driveway, I stopped the car, drove forward, and parked in front of the garage. I then jumped out and went inside, finding Ralph sitting in the hallway as though he was expecting me. After petting him on the head, I returned to the car.

"He's fine," I said, putting the car into reverse again.

"Wait, wait... are you sure he's OK?" she asked.

I replied, "Yes, he's fine," but Renee insisted on running back inside to check for herself. When she returned, I asked, "Did you lock the door?" She was not 100% certain, so I got out to check and found that the door was indeed locked, but I decided to go back in the house to check on Ralph one more time. He was still sitting in the same spot in the middle of the hallway and probably wondering why we were still acting so obsessive... after five years.

RENEE AND I had become a bit paranoid whenever we left the house. The back door had to be double-checked to ensure it was locked and bolted. We weren't afraid of being robbed. Our real concern was that if someone broke into our house, Ralph would run to greet them. His joyful purring and docile, charming personality might entice the intruder to steal *him*, while ignoring our six-year-old big-screen TV and my world-wide collection of Starbucks coffee mugs.

RELAXING ON THE front porch one morning with my coffee and a newspaper, I noticed a young boy, perhaps three years old, walking with his mother. Suddenly, he stopped in front of our house and pointed up at the porch.

"Mommy... that's a baby lion!"

Despite the warm summer weather, Ralph was still sporting his winter coat and looking very regal with his bushy orange hair around his neck. Although many others had made the same "lion cub" observation, Ralph more closely resembled an adult male lion, shrunken in size, minus a roar, but with a very loud *meow*.

Living in the city of Madison among a quarter-million people, Renee and I feel fortunate that our house is located in the central Isthmus area, only a mile from the center of the city. On our street, all 25 houses face the 38-acre, picturesque Tenney Park with its splendid lagoon. This spacious and tranquil setting attracts a wide variety of birds including robins, cardinals, woodpeckers, hawks, ducks, geese, herons, and the occasional Sandhill cranes.

No wonder Ralph loved being out on our screened front

porch as often as possible. From early spring until late fall, the porch was Ralph's favorite area of the house. This was his paradise for napping or smelling the fresh air while observing people, their pets, and all of nature. Nothing could be better.

The porch juts out from the house and is quite large—19 feet long and 10 feet wide—with floor-to-ceiling redwood screens on three sides that offer a superb, 180-degree view. Since the house and porch were built five feet above grade, there is a wonderful overview of the sidewalk, twenty feet away, and of the park just across the street. Shaded by large overhangs, the porch was a wonderful oasis for the three of us to relax throughout all seasons except winter.

With a colorful assortment of potted flowers cascading down our front steps in the summer, people walking in the neighborhood would often stop to admire the blooms. On particularly bright days, it was difficult for them to see us sitting or napping on the porch, but we could clearly see and hear them.

"What wonderful flowers! And such a nice porch."

With his face against the screen, Ralph often greeted them with a friendly "meow," prompting another a response, "And they have such a nice cat."

Ralph's excitement and enthusiasm for "porch time" was insatiable. Any time we were preparing to go outside, we would say to him, "Porch, porch!" Just by the tone of our voices, he immediately ran to the front door and pressed his body tightly against the wall like a horse getting into the starting gate. No movement, no fidgeting, just patiently waiting for the door to open, and then he would burst across the threshold and onto the porch.

He would spend the whole day out there and most of the night, if we allowed it, and that created another challenging problem. He often refused to come back inside. That prompted Renee to coin the phrase, "Corral the Ruffie," as the two of us chased him around the porch while he used the furniture to his advantage. To avoid going inside, he'd flatten himself down and slip under the couch. Getting him to come out became so difficult that I suggested we needed a herding dog.

One evening while trying to coax him out, Renee and I had to carefully lift up the whole couch and move it aside, almost crushing him in the process. When this finally became too problematic, I jammed an assortment of empty boxes and plastic containers under the couch. The visual appearance was unsightly and did not go unnoticed when some acquaintances stopped by for a visit. As we stood on the porch chatting, their eyes went to the underside of the couch, leading to a sarcastic comment, "What's all *that*?"

They may have thought we were storing trash under the couch, but I didn't care. I felt we had a fine porch, even though it would never be featured in *Better Homes and Gardens*. Renee, on the other hand, was offended by their remarks and wished that Ralph had bitten them. Regardless of how it looked, we had another problem. Ralph was getting clever at nudging aside the smaller boxes to create just enough room to lodge himself underneath and refuse to come out. This usually played out around midnight when he suspected we were about to go inside. That's when he'd jump down and burrow under the couch, like a crab hiding between rocks. I needed a better solution.

I went to the sporting goods aisle of a nearby retailer and

returned home with an air mattress. My ingenious plan was to remove all the unsightly boxes and containers from under the couch, then slide the air mattress underneath, blow it up, and fill the void. This would leave no space for Ralph to hide at night.

While I was positioning the air mattress, Ralph perched on his plastic chair, intently watching me from just a few feet away. As I was about to inflate the mattress, I paused and said, "Sorry Ralph, no more *hidey-holes*." My remark may have been premature. Within a minute, my cheeks were incredibly sore. It was impossible for me to blow that much air through the valve, so I drove back to the store and bought an electric air pump.

When I returned, Renee was on the porch reading a book and Ralph was beside her with his head on her lap. The noise from the air pump struck him like a lightning bolt, sending him scurrying inside the house as the air mattress started to inflate. The open space underneath the couch was filling up nicely. I was thrilled, until the whole couch started rising off the floor, like too much yeast in dough. Reversing the pump, I muttered a few words when I realized I had released too much air. My next attempt went well, until I noticed I overinflated the back side, which pushed the couch away from the wall. I had to release more air, readjust the couch, and then reinflate the air mattress.

During the entire time, Ralph's head was visible in the doorway, his eyes curiously watching me and studying my progress. Once I was done and put away the *scary* pump, he wandered outside for an inspection. When Renee saw my finished work, her first comment was, "Who in the world has an air mattress bulging out from under their couch?" She was actually teasing me. She really didn't care how it looked, just as long as it worked.

Ralph was quick to notice the change and he repeatedly scouted the front and sides of the couch looking for ways underneath. Convinced it was impenetrable, he snuggled between us on the couch, and all was well. Once again, I felt I had outsmarted Ralph, but he never let me savor victory for long. Toward midnight, he got up from the couch and walked across Renee's lap. Instead of jumping down to explore for moths and bugs, he climbed up on the back of the couch and promptly vanished. We heard nothing, just sensed his disappearance, and then Renee realized that he'd fallen into the narrow space between the top of the couch and the brick wall behind it.

Fortunately, the air mattress behind the couch had cushioned his fall, but he was probably still processing that he was trapped. The space was too narrow for him to climb out and impossible for us to lift him out. Our only recourse was to deflate the air mattress and pull the couch away from the wall. Once our scared *boy* was safely in Renee's arms, we went directly to bed.

In the morning, after repositioning the couch and reinflating the air mattress, I bought a dozen foam noodles and filled in all the spaces behind the couch. I was proud of my ingenuity, until Renee pointed out that I had inadvertently knocked the electronic temperature gauge off the windowsill, causing it to fall behind the couch, completely out of reach.

For the fourth time, I deflated the air mattress and pulled the couch away from the wall. All the noodles that had been lodged so precisely cascaded onto the floor. I wanted to cry.

Putting everything back in place—the couch, the air mattress, and all the foam noodles—took more than an hour. To prevent a recurrence, I taped the temperature gauge to the windowsill.

Our nights on the porch were again peaceful and pleasant, with Ralph alerting us to any sightings of rabbits, opossums, and raccoons that meandered across the front yard in the darkness. Despite the redundancy of saying "things were back to normal," they never were. Within a week, Ralph was again underneath the couch—the air mattress somehow went flat. Whether it was defective or punctured by *someone's* jaws, It didn't matter. I had anticipated something like this happening and had the foresight to purchase *two* air mattresses. My only regret was not buying three.

After several summers in Madison, Renee and I agreed that we had no desire for scenic getaways to northern Wisconsin. We considered our porch to be like a vacation spot or even a second home. With the wonderful park across the street, we often felt we were residing in a peaceful, countryside atmosphere while also living in the heart of the city.

Every Saturday morning from mid-April until the end of September, Renee and I would leave the house early and go to the downtown farmers' market, the largest producers-only market in the U.S.

During our typical hour-long stroll, we filled shopping bags with a variety of fresh produce, cheese curds, bakery items, sweet corn, apples, honey, potted plants, and wonderful flower bouquets. Returning home was the best part because Ralph was always waiting for us in his window perch. Once our bounty was put away, the fun began. We brewed shots of espresso for iced coffees, gathered newspapers, pastries, and fruit, and then headed out to the porch with Ralph leading the way. Once there, he raced to the screens or onto his yellow gardening mat, intent on watching passersby or focusing on the chipmunks and birds that knew they were safe on the *other* side of the screens.

As noon approached, Renee typically abandoned us to take a long walk. Returning two hours later, she was never surprised to find Ralph and me still relaxing on the porch. When the weather cooperated, *every day* was becoming a porch day, not just Saturdays. But at dusk, a transformation took place outside. The park across the street entered its quiet phase when pedestrian and car traffic slowed to a trickle. Our evenings on the porch became much more tranquil.

All the chirping birds, chipmunks, and squirrels settled down for the night, and a host of different creatures took their place in the dark, quiet surroundings. While the screens protected us from biting insects, Ralph watched and listened intently for any sign of a passing neighbor cat or other creatures.

To take full advantage of these beautiful nights, I suggested to Renee that we go camping, something she had never experienced in her entire life. Best of all, there was no need to drive long distances on crowded highways. We also didn't need to buy sleeping bags and a tent, or rent a cabin on a lake. Instead, I introduced her to what I called "porch camping."

On less humid summer nights, we'd haul our "camping equipment" out the front door and onto the porch. Most of our gear consisted of basic household items such as blankets, pillows, flashlights, cell phones, books, battery-powered book lights, bottles of water, snacks, and a three-inch-thick foam pad to put over the couch cushions. The cooler the evening temperatures, the cozier and more comfortable we were.

We seldom turned on the overhead porch light, preferring to snuggle together with just our reading lights. During these calm and tranquil evenings, chirping crickets conducted a symphony that lulled us into a deep slumber. It was difficult to remain awake past midnight, so we would set aside our books and stretch out on the couch in total darkness, with Ralph choosing to lie on top of us. Covered with his thin baby blanket, only his radar-like ears were visible, and for a good reason.

He often woke from a deep sleep and low-crawled to the front screens, sensing some type of animal lurking in the darkness. On one moonless night, Ralph popped his head up from the blankets, sat motionless and alert for a moment, and then jumped down, pacing back and forth in front of the screens. We heard and saw nothing, but Ralph was quite agitated. Suddenly, Renee untangled herself from the blankets and got on her feet, scooping up Ralph and carrying him inside the house. I gathered everything else and quickly followed. Although we couldn't see what Ralph heard or saw, we didn't care. We just knew it was a skunk.

On another evening as we were dozing far past midnight, Ralph woke up and cautiously approached the screens, freezing in place and looking downward. As I focused my eyes on the black abyss five feet below us, I saw it, too. It was a large fox. I shook Renee awake, finger to my lips, as we silently marveled at this beautiful creature, until two inebriated young women came staggering down the sidewalk in the darkness, both laughing and talking loudly.

Instead of running away, the fox hurried into our neighbor's bushes. After the women passed, the fox came out and wandered into our back yard, probably hunting for rabbits. A few minutes later, it returned to the front yard, just below the porch, and then moved away. The backlighting from the lone streetlight in the park clearly outlined the fox as it casually pranced down the sidewalk, like a dog without an owner, and then it disappeared from view. Our proximity to the park afforded us these nighttime animal sightings, all thanks to Ralph. His keen vision and acute sense of hearing alerted us to these experiences.

I find it ironic that when I purchased the house in 1982, long before my move to Boston and two decades before I met Renee, I went through entire summers without ever sitting on the front porch. My only reason for buying the house was because of its location, only five blocks from my former workplace.

And then Renee and Ralph entered my life, opening my eyes and attuning my senses to the wonders of nature and the scenic beauty of the park across the street, all of which I had previously ignored. Surrounded by such an abundance of bird and animal activity, our home had become a special place for us, and a cat's paradise for Ralph. However, Renee had a much broader interpretation. She forever referred to our front and back yards as "The Mild Kingdom." And I knew that Ralph certainly agreed.

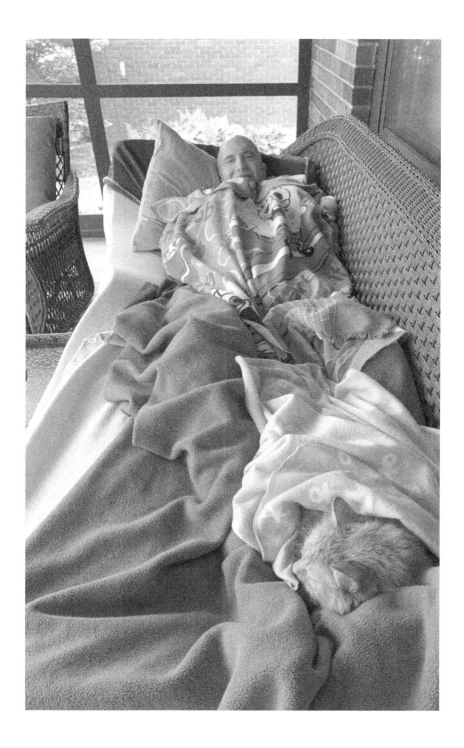

THIRTEEN

What's for dinner?

WHILE REPAIRING THE light fixture in the kitchen, I had to fetch a screwdriver from the basement and inadvertently left the door open for just a few seconds. Hearing me go downstairs, Ralph ran down and slipped past me to explore and hide among the tools, workbenches, shelving, and lumber. After 20 minutes of unsuccessfully searching for him, from one end of the basement to the other, I went upstairs to ask for Renee's help.

Imagine my surprise when I found her reading a book on the couch with Ralph quietly lying next to her. She said he must have slipped by me again because he had been with her for the last 15 minutes. Then she asked if I remembered to close the door. As I walked downstairs to do just that, Ralph raced past me into the basement once again. At this point, there was only one thing I could do. "Reneeeeee... come downstairs and find *your* cat."

PESKY SQUIRRELS FREQUENTLY invaded our bird feeders, gorging on seeds and suet, while Ralph's bird friends had to move aside and wait for them to leave. To deal with this ongoing problem, Ralph and I developed a team approach to *hunt* squirrels. He would lie down on the window perch with his nose pressed up against the screen. While he distracted them, I slowly opened the back door, just enough to slip the barrel of my gun through the crack, and then "bang, bang, bang."

Actually, the sound was more like "poof, poof, poof" from my Atomic Power Popper, a plastic toy gun approved for children aged four and up. It fired ten one-inch foam balls as fast as I could slide the pump-action lever. Although most of the balls missed their intended targets, a few harmlessly bounced off some very startled squirrels who ran off in all directions, while the birds immediately flocked back for brunch. Renee was not amused because she had to rummage through the flower beds, picking up all the foam balls. She often asked, "Was that really necessary?" If Ralph and the birds could speak, they would have replied, "Yes," and, "Thank you."

DURING ONE OF our frequent walks downtown to Starbucks, we had gone only two blocks when Renee asked me why I was limping. I explained I had a problem with my athletic sock. I thought it was bunched up inside my sneaker, so I bent down and gave it a firm tug. After another two blocks, I had to stop again, this time leaning on Renee as I took off my sneaker and carefully adjusted my sock again. Three steps later, Renee asked, "What is wrong with you?" I was really puzzled and also worried that I might have somehow injured my toe. After removing my sneaker a second time, I reached far inside the toe box and pulled out a foam ball that had tiny bite marks in it. Renee and I nodded in agreement, "Ralph!"

When we got home that afternoon, we finally understood why so many foam balls went missing. Ralph had been placing them in our shoes. As funny as that was, I never did figure out how one ball found its way inside the front pocket of my shorts, and Renee insisted she did not put it there.

RALPH SHOULD HAVE been a dog. Whenever anyone rang our doorbell, he immediately scampered ahead of us to be the first to greet whoever was at our front door: friend, neighbor, relative, delivery person, repair person, or anyone else. With such a curious and extroverted personality, Ralph always insisted on meeting, greeting, and interacting with everyone.

Over the years, I've heard stories from friends and acquaintances about their cats that had a tendency to run and hide whenever visitors came to their homes or apartments. Our friend Sarah, who is retired and living in Maine, has had a total of 11 wonderful and cherished cats throughout her life, and all of them initially ran and hid whenever guests came for a visit.

Renee is quick to note that shy cats are not bad cats. Quite often, cats simply feel safer and more secure among familiar faces. As for Ralph, we referred to him as the "Welcome Wagon cat" because he looked forward to visitors, both familiar faces and strangers alike. He feared no one and loved everyone, and we used that to our advantage. On those occasions when we couldn't immediately locate Ralph in the house, we simply opened the front door and rang the doorbell. Within seconds, he came scurrying to meet our visitors, only to be disappointed to see that it was just us.

After adopting Ralph, I assumed that feeding him would be easy. Just grab any bag of dry food and be on our way, until I saw how many varieties were stacked on the shelves at PetSmart. The categories and options were staggering: healthy nutrition, indoor adult, sensitive stomach, weight management, complete plan, pro-plan, urinary control, hairball control, kitten formula, balanced diet, healthy mix, smart blend, and gourmet adult, to name just a few.

While I was trying to make a decision, Renee reached up on a shelf and pulled down a ten-pound bag of dry food, "kibble" as she called it, adding, "This one is just fine." I had forgotten that she grew up with cats all her life and was well versed in cat food. She had clearly made a great choice—Ralph dug into his kibble with such gusto. He loved it. But now that his food requirements were satisfied, I felt he needed a better bowl.

I initially loaned him my old cereal bowl and soon up-graded to a higher-quality ceramic bowl from the Dollar Store. But his one-gallon watering station was a disappoint-ment. Too much of his long shedding hair was constantly pooling in the water, so we bought six more ceramic bowls and refreshed his water several times each day. A month later, we purchased an inexpensive gravity-operated kibble feeder. Just fill it and forget it, but after it plugged up a few times, it went into the trash. Besides, the ceramic bowls were inter-changeable for food and water. What could be simpler?

Ralph continued to enjoy his kibble, but insisted that his bowl be replenished every morning at 3 a.m., despite it never being empty. Renee devised a novel way of fooling him. She pretended to put more kibble into his bowl by picking it up and briefly setting it on the counter, then putting it back down on the floor. Ralph would look in his bowl, take a few mouthfuls, and go back to bed, satisfied that he was being properly fed.

After Ralph's first year with us, I felt we should give him something special for his birthday, perhaps some "mice cream." When the laughter subsided, I suggested a can of flaked tuna. Ralph loved it, licking his bowl clean and begging for more, while ignoring his presents: six toy mice and a balloon. I sug-gested we buy more canned food, but Renee reminded me of the adage, "Why ruin a good thing?" She said that for a reason, sensing I wanted to tamper with his eating habits.

On our next trip to the grocery store, I purchased three more cans of flaked tuna, still not aware that I was creat-ing an unnecessary headache for us. Ralph now seemed less interested in his kibble after tasting the *good stuff.* To clarify matters, I called five cat owners and asked them what they fed their cats. Kibble? Wet food? A combination of both? If canned food, what size portion, how often, and at what time of the day? Among all the respondents, their answers varied greatly—no two were alike, and yet all these people claimed their cats were happy and content, which left me perplexed.

Always the pragmatist, Renee did not follow my logic. "Ralph loves his kibble," she remarked, "so why did you think there's a problem with his food?" Perhaps I really was creating a problem or even "humanizing" him a bit. What if my mother had fed me only cereal while I was growing up and never introduced me to steak and potatoes? I just assumed that Ralph would enjoy a larger variety of dining options, and all those pet food ads and commercials implied that I was correct.

As the weeks passed, I convinced Renee that we should buy more cans of wet food for Ralph. Once I got to the grocery store, I found the choices to be overwhelming. One name-brand producer had more than a dozen categories of canned cat food: classic, marinated, roasted, flaked, chunky, grilled, minced, morsels, natural, shredded, sliced, blends, and paté. If that was not mind-boggling enough, the "classic" category had so many flavors: chicken, cod-sole-shrimp, salmon and shrimp, seafood, liver and chicken, chicken and tuna, chopped grill, ocean whitefish, and tuna. Then there were all the "gravy lovers" varieties, and that sounded delicious, yet a bit odd. Gravy is traditionally associated with meat, but I never heard of seafood with gravy.

I naturally became curious about what exactly was in these cans, but without my reading glasses or a microscope, it was difficult to read the ingredients. The cans were small and the font size was tiny. It could have been written in hieroglyphics, and few would have noticed. As for the contents being safe to eat, the FDA does not mandate that pet food makers specify where the product originated. But there was one item on all the cans that stood out clearly—"Label printed in the U.S.A." However, I doubt Ralph wanted to eat the labels.

While I still had my doubts, Renee put several cans of tuna with gravy in our basket, reassuring me that it was safe. Months later, Ralph's vet calmed my fears, explaining that wet food is actually a great supplement to his dry food, providing needed moisture in his diet. I relaxed again, for a while.

On Christmas Eve, we gave Ralph a can of tuna with gravy and watched him devour it. He licked the bowl spotless, then licked his face, as though he had just eaten a bucket of Colonel Sander's original recipe. On my next trip to the grocery store, I bought ten more cans. Renee suggested that I was using canned food to curry Ralph's favor, but I reassured her there was no competition, and that he loved us both. She responded, "Then why insist that *you* always get to feed him his wet food?"

I suppose I may have wanted to be the *good guy*, sensing that Ralph was never going to like me as much as he liked Renee. Perhaps I really was trying to buy a little more love and affection. However, once Ralph was hooked on wet food, there was no turning back to a solo diet of dry kibble. Now he had to have both, and this led to some interesting grocery shopping.

After browsing the pet food aisle at a major retail store, I bought all the individual cans of tuna with gravy that were on the shelf. With at least 75 cans in our shopping cart, the people behind us at the register were agitated and upset when the cashier insisted on scanning *every* can. After that experience, I tended to buy only case lots, but some stores preferred to take the cans out of the boxes and stack them individually on the shelves or dump them into large wire bins. But why all these single cans? Who would buy only three or four cans at a time? Do most pet owners really want to visit the store several times a week to buy canned cat food?

On one occasion while I was at the grocery store loading dozens of cans of tuna into my cart, I noticed a woman standing next to me. She was carefully selecting about ten different varieties of canned cat food. I was curious, so I asked, "Does your cat really enjoy *all* those different flavors?"

She looked up and responded, "Not really. My cat is so finicky that I've never been able to figure out exactly what she really likes to eat, so I keep buying all these different kinds." Then she glanced into my shopping cart, with about 70 cans of tuna with gravy, and commented, "That's a lot of cans... so how many cats do you have?"

"Just one," I responded.

As she started to walk away, she turned back and said, "He must be a very big cat." But before I could answer, she added, "Or he must have quite a large appetite."

"Yes, our boy loves his tuna," I replied.

"You are very lucky that he likes what you give him," she said, as she flashed a lighthearted smile, "Do you want to trade cats?"

As I pushed the cart toward the checkout register, I realized how fortunate we were that Ralph loved his tuna... until the day when he decided he didn't, leaving us with a pantry full of unwanted cans. That forced an unexpected trip to the store where I pondered, "What would I want to eat if I were a cat?" A half-hour later, I chose "Tuna Florentine with Greens" which sounded like a dish I once had in Italy. Ralph loved it, so I returned the next day and bought a full case. Three days later, he decided he no longer enjoyed Italian food.

Over the following week, we allowed Ralph to sample a variety of canned foods, including beef, turkey, and chicken. He was underwhelmed, until Renee introduced him to the seafood categories and discovered a real winner with salmon paté. With his food issues resolved, life was back to normal for almost a full month until Ralph decided he had eaten too much salmon. Fortunately, our pantry still had dozens of cans of tuna and that Florentine stuff, so we tried an experiment. We began rotating the other flavors with his salmon, and Ralph finally appeared satisfied.

Now that I was retired, I had an abundance of time to sit on the porch with Ralph and search the Internet for feline facts and minutiae. One interesting story suggested that some food bowls could possibly irritate a cat's whiskers if the bowls were too small or too deep. Curious to know if this was fact or fiction, I got down on my hands and knees, and watched Ralph eating his wet food. A minute later, Renee wandered into the kitchen and asked why Ralph and I had our faces planted over his food bowl. I explained that I needed to observe him closely because I suspected his bowl might be irritating his whiskers and causing a problem. Renee remarked that maybe *I* was the problem.

But I really did notice that Ralph had trouble eating his

wet food from the small ceramic bowls. He often had to push the tuna up the side of the bowl with his tongue and work hard to get his last licks. My solution was to serve Ralph his canned food on our new Crate and Barrel salad plates, with a special twist. I set the plate on top of the bowl. The added height from the floor meant that Ralph didn't have to bend his head as much to enjoy his dinner. It seemed perfectly logical to me, but Renee suggested that if I found that so enticing, she would happily place my dinner plate on the floor next to his.

While Ralph continued to be a finicky eater, my brother John's all-black domestic shorthair, Smokey, loved *fresh* fish and certainly lived in the right house. John happens to be an avid fisherman. Every time he returned home with a successful catch, he delighted in waking Smokey by calmly enunciating the word "fish-ies." Hearing that, Smokey was up in an instant, running across the living room, down the basement stairs, and jumping up onto John's custom-built cleaning station where he had already placed his freshly caught perch or walleyes. After quickly gutting and trimming each fish into two fillets, he stacked them next to Smokey who was fixated like the statue of the *Maltese Falcon,* but alive and waiting.

In the final step of filleting the meat from the skin, John would slice off generous tidbits for his hungry, enthusiastic companion. After cleaning up the area, he took the fillets directly to the kitchen to be breaded and fried, while Smokey returned to his fluffy pillow next to the fireplace to await his next meal.

I suspect most cats would relish freshly caught fish, but not Ralph. When I once offered him a morsel of lake perch, he licked it a few times and walked away, preferring to wait for his daily offering of canned salmon or tuna. It was obvious that he was becoming very spoiled. He even started lapping up water from *our* glasses when they were full, rather than drinking from his bowl. Perhaps the latter had something to do with whisker interference? I told Renee I should do a research paper on the topic. She suggested that I go out on the porch and take a nap with Ralph.

FOURTEEN

Who's watching Ralph?

ON THE DAY Renee flew back to visit her parents for a week, I remained home with Ralph and decided to buy and enjoy a whole pre-cooked chicken from our local grocery store. During the drive home, my taste buds were salivating with delight. With such a large bird, there was no need for side dishes such as vegetables or potatoes. My entire meal would consist of *just chicken*.

After carefully transferring the chicken to a platter, I left it on the dining room table and went to get a magazine, napkins, and a beverage. When I returned, Ralph was on the table vigorously licking one side of the bird and still undecided if his first bite should be a drumstick or a thigh. I shooed him away, but he merely stepped across to his window perch and lay down, facing me, while I started carving the bird. As I began to eat, I noticed a pair of sad, round eyes quietly staring at me.

"OK, Ralph... come over and have some." He understood. Soon we were both enjoying chicken at the dining room table.

I cut his portions into small manageable pieces, and he relished each bite. "Don't tell Mom," I said, knowing Renee would not have approved, and then I thought out loud, "Should we have prime rib tomorrow night?" And we did!

AS I WAS backing the car out of our driveway, I happened to look up on the front porch and immediately slammed on the brakes. Ralph's expressive face was pressed against the porch screen door, watching me abandon him. Apparently, I forgot to take him back inside after I finished my morning coffee. For safety and security reasons, he was never allowed to be on the porch alone. And since Renee had already gone for a walk, this was totally my fault. I would be in serious trouble *if* she ever found out about my negligence. After I ushered Ralph back inside the house, I gave him several tasty tuna treats, and I vowed that I would never again be so careless.

Several months later, I was replacing our back door when Ralph apparently walked right past me and out into the back yard. I was shocked when I happened to look up and see him lying on the grass. After rushing to pick him up and carry him back inside, I felt so relieved that he hadn't run away. Considering my previous Ralph-related offensives, I had no intention of telling Renee. This would remain another secret until the statute of limitations ran out.

RALPH OFTEN ENJOYED jumping into the top drawer of my dresser while I put away my freshly laundered T-shirts and socks. My problem was that I could not coax him out. He was so stubborn, letting his body go limp like a bowling ball without finger holes, leaving me only one option. "Reneeeeee... I need your help!" Renee is an expert at cat extractions but, unfortunately, she was outside in the garden and couldn't hear me. As I hovered over Ralph, he burrowed in deeper, like a flounder, while slipping his head under several pairs of socks. He had no intention of moving.

Ignoring a possible censure from the ASPCA, I decided to scare him just a little by slowly closing the dresser drawer, counting to twenty, and then slowly sliding it back open. No response, no fear. He was already fast asleep and confident that I would never do anything to harm him, and he was correct. But I did have one last option. With a sly grin on my face, I walked into the hallway and started down the stairs, calling out behind me, "Ralph, Ralph... food, food!" Before I got to the bottom of the stairs, he raced past me and went directly to his food bowl. Manipulating him with tuna or salmon was easy, as long as he wasn't outside on the front porch where food enticements never worked.

GARBAGE TRUCKS AND thunder were Ralph's Achilles' paw. He especially feared the latter, so when a fierce thunderstorm rolled in one night, he and Renee huddled together on the couch. As midnight approached, the tornado sirens

started blaring, and our local weatherperson on TV was confirming that a tornado had been sighted over the center of the
city. "If you live just east of the Capitol, you have only one
minute to take shelter," the announcer firmly warned.

Renee jumped up and headed for our basement, calling
for me to follow. We had only seconds to grab one important item. She chose Ralph, while I picked up my laptop bag.
Halfway down the basement stairs, I stopped and ran back up
to the kitchen, stuffing two bananas and four cans of cat food
in the hip pockets of my shorts. As I started down the stairs
again, I could hear the updated report on TV confirming that
the funnel cloud was directly over our neighborhood.

Renee was upset that I had gone back upstairs, until I
showed her the bananas and the cans of tuna. I explained that
in the event of catastrophic damage, we could make the bananas last for two days, while Ralph could last for more than
a week... as long as I survived to open the cans for him. Such
levity on my part did not make for good humor under those
circumstances.

Fortunately, the small funnel cloud missed our house by
six blocks and caused minimal damage in the area. After we
came up from the basement, we enjoyed a late-night snack,
eating both bananas and giving Ralph a whole can of tuna.
We then agreed that it would be prudent to always have some
emergency supplies on hand. Within a month, our basement
was stockpiled with four flashlights, extra batteries, assorted
canned goods, a supply of bottled water, and most importantly, three cases of canned cat food.

WHEN A UPS box arrived one day, I immediately peeled off the tape and opened the carton, while a curious Ralph stepped across to the dining room table from his window perch and peeked inside. I called out to Renee, "Wow... come and look at this."

After glancing inside, she said sarcastically, "That's what you're so excited about?"

The box contained a full case of Victor Corporation's finest mouse traps, 16 individual packets of four. I touted these as the best among all brands, considering that more than *one billion* had been sold over the past century. After removing one of the plastic-wrapped packets from the box and setting it on the table, Ralph cautiously pawed it a few times and then slapped it onto the floor. He obviously didn't like them.

After I closed and resealed the box, Renee told me to put them away until I needed them for next fall's annual mouse migration. But six months later, when I went to retrieve the traps, I forgot where I had put them. An exhaustive search of the basement and the second-floor storeroom was fruitless. The traps were gone, perhaps tossed out by mistake. Renee looked at me and shook her head. "Don't blame me or Ralph," she said. "Your box of traps is still sitting on the dining room floor. You never did put the box away." I suppose I walked past it so often that I no longer noticed it. However, if Ralph had done *his* job, we would never have needed those traps.

Several years later, the humor was gone after the mice took their revenge on our car. They chewed through the wiring under the engine compartment, rendering the vehicle inoperable and causing $650 damage. The result was that I now hated mice a lot more than I once disliked cats.

When we adopted Ralph, I never factored in the need for a pet sitter if we still intended to fulfill our long-awaited dreams of travel and adventure. I also recall chatting with a friend who explained that he and his wife were often away for a full week, and they left their cat at home alone with no problems. I was somewhat relieved to hear that, but Renee was highly skeptical of his claim and sensed he was exaggerating. Another cat owner explained that before he went away on any trips, he lined up the appropriate number of bowls of kibble based on how many days he would be gone. I found that incredulous. Was his cat so brilliant that it could count the bowls and measure its daily intake?

Previously, I had never considered the need for a pet sitter because I never visualized owning a cat. Six months before adopting Ralph, we had already booked a four-day trip to Albuquerque. However, Renee felt strongly that being away from home for more than two days would necessitate having someone come into our house to refresh Ralph's food and water bowls, and provide some human contact. She also insisted that if Ralph didn't have a sitter, I would be traveling by myself, and she would be staying home with him.

With only three weeks until our planned departure, I sought solace from my longtime friend Don, who totally surprised me by revealing that he had two cats of his own. He explained that he got them many years earlier for his young sons, but once they grew up and left home, the cats remained. After listening to my plight, Don graciously offered to help. He said he would be happy to drive across town every night after work to care for Ralph. Our vacation was back on schedule!

When Renee and I arrived home from our trip, Don explained that his visits with Ralph had been great fun. Ralph greeted him at the door every night, and then Don would replenish his kibble, refresh his water, and scoop his poop. Afterward, he sat at the dining room table for an hour reading news magazines, while Ralph lay on the table next to him the whole time. Weeks later, while I was treating Don to lunch, he admitted that one night while he was caring for Ralph, he fell asleep on our couch after a long day at work. When he woke up, he found Ralph sleeping on his chest. Following that experience, Don always referred to Ralph as "my new little buddy."

Although we appreciated Don taking such great care of Ralph, we also realized that we had to find a pet sitter who lived much closer to us. Fortunately, one of my sisters knew a nurse in our neighborhood whose teenage daughter did babysitting. That circuitous route was how Ralph met his new sitter, Greta, who lived only a few blocks away and liked cats. She and Ralph got along extremely well, providing us the confidence to book more vacations. Over the next 18 months, Renee and I were traveling often and enjoying it immensely. Then Greta informed us that she'd be going away to college.

What were we going to do now, considering that we had already booked a number of future trips? The thought of substituting an eight-day excursion to Japan and a trip to Rome for a day trip to some nearby tourist town was very depressing. Renee insisted there must be pet sitters in our area and that we just needed to look harder. As it turned out, "The Fates" were kind to us once again.

During the summer of 2013, a family from Washington, D.C., moved into our neighborhood, only five houses away from ours. We first met Angie and Mary late one night when they saw us sitting on the front porch and asked if we had seen their buff-colored tabby who had somehow slipped out of their house. Renee and I immediately joined the search, walking around the block several times until we spotted Angie waving to us with the happy news. Their cat Chessie had *not* escaped. She'd been hiding deep inside their closet, still struggling with the adjustment to her new home.

During a casual conversation a few days later, we were overjoyed to discover that Angie was a full-time, professional pet sitter, following ten years in the Army as a captain in the Signal Corps. She had worked in vet clinics and had 24 years of experience caring for dogs and cats and, depending on the season, she also handled snow shoveling and plant watering. I was thrilled. I didn't know whether to hug her, salute her, or both.

Angie's initial meet-and-greet with Ralph went smoothly. He boldly introduced himself and never left her side as she took notes on our emergency contacts and vet information. According to Angie, they bonded immediately and enjoyed each other's company.

"He is so charismatic and unique," she said after getting to know him. "I would see him in the window, waiting for me, even before I finished turning the key in the lock. He was always there to greet me at the back door."

Angie also mentioned that if she was doing something in our back yard, such as watering plants or shoveling snow, Ralph would sit in his window perch and watch her until she came inside. After an enthusiastic greeting, he led her to the kitchen where she prepared his bowl of canned tuna while he repeatedly rubbed against the back of her legs as a way of saying, "Hurry up with that food." In the winter months, they retired to the TV room where Ralph always sat next to her, snugged tightly against her leg, while she watched TV. During warmer weather, he typically led her to the front door so they could go out on the porch and sit together on the couch. Ralph thoroughly enjoyed her company and was always sad to see her leave.

Throughout her lengthy career of pet sitting, Angie estimated that she had cared for over 300 cats and many more dogs, and admitted that she had never met a cat like Ralph, so docile and friendly. Her favorite nickname for him was "Mr. Personality," and she added, "Ralph was the only cat that I loved as if he were my own." That was, indeed, a wonderful and sincere compliment. With Angie and Ralph such bonded friends, Renee and I could always leave home with no worries, other than missing him.

Looking back at Ralph's first year with us, I am deeply ashamed that I had instructed Greta to visit Ralph "once every two or three days" when we were away for weeks. Renee insisted that intermittent visits were *not* often enough. Angie was also in agreement with Renee, and she visited Ralph *every day*. We even asked her to extend some of her daily visits a bit longer, not realizing that she was already doing that, often on her own time.

Now that Ralph was safe, happy, and comfortable in our home under Angie's watchful care, Renee and I were again going on some wonderful overseas trips. However, when we were at home for the other ten months of the year, we doted on Ralph, spending vast amounts of time with him, day and night. He followed us everywhere throughout the house and never tired of our company while performing his "feline magic" on us. As our attachment to him grew, he was no longer a mere pet. He had become an integral member of our family.

In hindsight, I never did change Ralph's bad habits the way I intended. Instead, it was Ralph who converted me into a fervent cat lover, and I eventually came around to love him very much.

My friend Don was Ralph's first pet sitter.

FIFTEEN

The Mild Kingdom

AFTER ACCIDENTALLY LEAVING the bathroom door open one morning, I found a broken clay flowerpot on the tile floor, dirt scattered everywhere, and the plant was missing. I realized that Ralph must have swallowed it—a five-inch cactus completely covered with tiny thorns. I worried that he might need a costly trip to the ER for a checkup, X-rays, and maybe even surgery. Renee calmed me down and pointed out that cats often swallow their prey whole. Fortunately, Ralph had no digestive issues, but I now felt that plants with thorns did not belong in a house with a cat.

AS WE RELAXED on the porch one afternoon, our mail carrier, Ryan, walked up the front steps and handed Renee a package from a New York publishing company. After ripping it open, she got all excited and said, "Wow... Ralph is famous!" The enclosed letter explained that Ralph had been chosen for a page in the 2016 desktop edition of the "365 Days" cat calendar. Included in the package was a free calendar. Quickly thumbing through the pages, Renee found his picture on September 5, Labor Day. She had forgotten that two years earlier she submitted photos of Ralph to the publisher for consideration. Someone must have thought Ralph very photogenic— he was selected to appear two more times, in 2017 and 2020, but they continued to list him as "Age 5."

Ralph's reputation for being a rascal must have caught the editors' attention. In his next two calendar appearances, he was selected for the "Bad Cat" version which would have been more appropriate during his earlier years with us, before he surprisingly settled down and reformed.

RENEE WALKED INTO the kitchen and almost tripped over us. Ralph was in the middle of the room with his head lowered. I was kneeling behind him with the palms of my hands on either side of his body and my head directly behind his. "What are you guys doing?" she asked.

I immediately responded, "Don't come in here, we're busy." She walked away laughing when she realized the object of our intense focus was a tiny spider, the size of a pinhead, zigzagging erratically on the floor in front of us. Ralph was actually afraid of spiders, but he loved to observe them. When the little arachnid started moving quickly toward his paw,

Ralph jumped backwards, banging the back of his head into my chin. That was enough. I got up and finished breakfast, Ralph went back to his perch to watch birds, and the spider eventually made it to safety under the dishwasher.

Despite being an indoor cat, Ralph had plenty of animal friends in the neighborhood, even though he couldn't go outside to play with them. His extroverted personality always found a way around this dilemma, and one of his first face-to-face encounters happened shortly after he came to live with us.

One morning as I was leaving the house, Mikki, our small neighbor cat, was hanging out by our back door and popped her head across the threshold. Unbeknownst to me, Ralph had followed me down the back stairs and stretched his head past my leg, touching his nose to hers as they acknowledged each other like old friends. No hissing and no signs of fear. I was quite surprised. On the flip side, Mikki's feline housemate, "Big Bill," was the alpha cat in the neighborhood and very territorial.

Although Mikki became Ralph's first cat friend, we decided it was best not to let them come into direct contact. Mikki was primarily an outdoor cat, and Ralph was strictly an indoor boy, so no play dates. But there were many nights when Mikki would come up the front steps and sit by the screen door as we sat on the porch. Ralph always jumped off the couch and ran to greet her, even lying next to her, with only the screen separating them.

On misty or rainy nights, Mikki would seek refuge under our porch overhang to shelter from the elements. It was sad when it was time for us to gather our belongings and go inside. Mikki had to stay and wait for the rain to stop before returning home. To rectify that situation, I built her a waterproof shelter and placed it in the back yard next to the garage. During inclement weather, we often saw her lying in the shelter with only her bright eyes visible against her black fur. In the morning, seeing our faces in the window, she would dash up the brick walkway to the back door for a breakfast bowl of canned tuna.

Despite having a loving home just a few houses away, Mikki spent a considerable amount of time in our back yard, pausing during her daily ramblings through the neighborhood to lie next to our flower beds or beneath Ralph's window perch. When Renee was gardening, Mikki often enjoyed hanging out with her. That provided double entertainment for Ralph, who got to observe the two of them while trying to get their attention with repeated "meows." Mikki was such a delightful, friendly cat, and had grown very close to us, which made it more difficult when her owners announced that they were moving overseas. Then they asked us if we wanted to adopt her.

We already knew that Mikki and Ralph got along very well, but she had always been an outdoor cat. Her owners had explained that she insisted on going outside, so forcing her to stay indoors, against her will, would not work. Sadly, Renee and I had to decline. After Mikki's departure, our appreciation for having Ralph in our lives grew that much stronger, as did our tendency to hug him more often for no apparent reason.

On an unusually warm day in late February, a beautiful

gray cat casually approached me outside, directly under our dining room window. Ralph had been sitting on his perch, excited and alert, with his face pressed against the glass. He was very aware of the cat's presence as he watched me bend down and pet this unknown, velveteen feline on the head.

According to the collar, her name was Gracie. She was docile and friendly and even allowed me pick her up—no hissing or hesitation. That was surprising, considering my past history with cats. As she followed me to the back door, I called to Renee who immediately rushed outside with tuna treats. Ralph also ran to the door, offering Gracie a nose-to-nose greeting. He now had a new friend, and they got along well together. But where did she come from? Renee already knew every cat in the neighborhood and didn't recognize her.

Throughout the week, Gracie visited us every day. We definitely wanted to adopt her but, after making some inquires, I discovered that she and her owner were temporarily staying with a friend just a few houses away. That house had four small dogs, so Gracie found it less stressful and more relaxing to be outside during the day, even in cold weather, rather than being cooped up in a bedroom with dogs barking outside her door.

For the next several months, Gracie frequently stopped to pay us a visit and enjoy some treats. Ralph was so intrigued that he would sit in the window and not take his eyes off her until she meandered away. But in the spring Gracie's owner informed us that they were moving back to Kentucky. We were extremely sad to see them go, yet life continued on in the "Mild Kingdom."

"There's activity outside!" Ralph spoke using his tail, sweeping it back and forth with great excitement and enthusiasm. If there were birds or chipmunks outside, Ralph would flatten himself down on his perch, concealing all but his eyes and ears. With larger animals such as squirrels, ducks, opossums, or raccoons, he preferred to sit upright for a better view, eagerly observing their every movement. However, there was one animal that really raised Ralph's adrenaline level: another cat. It would set his tail wagging as though it might snap off at any moment. Yet Ralph never hissed or exhibited aggression, just interest and curiosity, and a desire for friendly interaction.

After Big Bill, the local alpha male, had moved away, a newcomer soon arrived and immediately started patrolling the neighborhood. He was a lean, fit, short-haired gray male. Renee nicknamed him "Earl Gray," or "Earl" for short. We often joked that Earl Gray was the cousin of the Sheriff of Nottingham, and that Ralph was a distant relative of Robin Hood, characters that matched their personalities. Unfortunately, we had no idea which neighborhood castle "The Earl" resided in.

Several months later, we discovered that Earl lived on the street behind ours, just one house away. His daily routine involved jumping his fence, passing behind our garage, and venturing through our back yard. This way he avoided the neighbor dogs on both sides of our lot and gained easy access to the park across the street. Since Earl preferred our yard as his main thoroughfare, we saw him on a regular basis. He was shy, yet streetwise, and always kept his distance, until our frequent offerings of kibble or canned tuna helped earn his trust. We were amazed at how fast he could eat. He'd consume a whole can of food as if it had been his only meal of the day, but his owners assured me that he was very well fed at home.

I had my doubts, until Renee showed me an article about

cats being opportunistic eaters. They will often two-time their owners by accepting extra food from neighbors. That made sense, considering how often we looked outside in the mornings and saw Earl sitting on our back stoop, waiting patiently, as though he had taken a number at the local deli. When he saw our faces in the window, he got so excited knowing he was about to receive another meal. Being outside all day, he obviously burned a lot of calories. He also had no *fat pan* under his belly, unlike Ralph.

Over the years, our continued affection for Earl, whose real name was "Ben," grew immensely. He became much more friendly and trusting toward Renee and me, but he still disliked all other cats. As he passed through our yard multiple times a day, he would hiss at Ralph who was in his window or on the porch. Ralph never hissed back, not even once. All Ralph wanted was another friend.

Aside from Earl and the avian community that flocked to our bird feeders, Ralph's summer interest was watching chipmunks. They entertained him for hours, but they also caused extensive damage to our flower beds and garden. Some were so bold that they'd scurry up the front steps and dig up the soil in our flowerpots, despite a pair of large yellow eyes fixated on them from only a few feet away. Only the safety of the porch screens separated them from Ralph, and they knew it.

We heard many stories from irate homeowners who trapped chipmunks because of their destructive nature. I was considering such a measure, until we had the "incident." One evening as we were watering plants, Renee called for my help. In her strawberry patch, a small chipmunk was tangled in the nylon netting and desperately gasping for air. I immediately ripped the net off the stakes, while Renee hurried inside to get her sewing scissors. After flipping the chipmunk onto its back, I carefully snipped the nylon netting that was cinched noose-like around its neck. Within seconds it was free, and our net ruined, but we were all happy.

Directly above me in the window, Ralph observed the entire operation with keen interest. As soon as I set the chipmunk on the ground, the little critter burst to life, running willy-nilly into the farthest depths of our garden. As Renee and I waved goodbye, Ralph let loose a salvo of "meows." Saving a life is much more satisfying than trapping one, unless it involves mice.

Several years later, we had another emergency. This time a chipmunk had chewed through the rubber gasket on the bottom of the garage door and was partially caught in a mouse trap. I immediately donned a pair of plastic surgical gloves, the ones I used for painting, and made preparations to free it. However, the chipmunk was huge and feisty, and squirming wildly. This was obviously going to be a difficult surgery. While holding the patient in the palm of my left hand, I was surprised when it suddenly turned its head and sank its teeth into my forefinger, biting hard and refusing to let go.

"Renee... Renee..." I was screaming for help as I ran out of the garage with a giant chipmunk dangling from my fingertip and the trap still attached to its tail and back leg. Renee raced outside, looked at my predicament and said there was nothing she could do. With a sigh of pity, she turned around and walked back into the house. I was on my own, and sadly, there was no happy outcome this time.

After thoroughly washing my wound, I spent an hour reading internet articles to assess if I needed to get a rabies shot. I also learned a valuable lesson. I was not a wildlife rehab expert, and I would not make a good surgeon. Renee said later that Ralph had not watched this fiasco. Instead, he was sound asleep on the window perch with his stuffed animals, and perhaps that was for the best.

Redemption followed months later when another chipmunk slipped into the garage and also got caught in a mousetrap. Renee went back inside; she didn't want to watch. This little *chipper* was struggling for its life, so I had to act immediately. With no gloves, I used my "cat technique," gripping it firmly by the nape of its neck, using only my thumb and forefinger. With my other hand, I was able to delicately free its tail. After I placed it on the ground, the much-relieved creature ran off and dove into the nearest hole. Renee later said that Ralph had been watching the entire episode from his window perch.

I was done worrying about chipmunks, but the following spring we had a new challenge. Ralph's swishing tail would alert us to herds of rabbits that appeared every day in the back yard. Their antics were amazing to watch. Running, hopping, leaping, cavorting, and circling each other, all part of their courting rituals. About a month and a half later, little bunnies, or "micro-hares," as Renee called them, started popping out of the hosta garden to nibble on grasses, clover and, of course, our dainty plants.

Ralph enjoyed watching the bunnies and would race through the house, skidding around corners on the hardwood floors and going from one window to another to seek a better vantage point. It was the cuteness of these little *hoppers* that spared them from Renee's wrath. Year after year, they mowed down many of her favorite flowers and plants. But as long as Ralph was enthralled with their playfulness, she didn't mind.

Our friend Earl Gray… his real name was Ben.

SIXTEEN

Lost and found

EVERY WEDNESDAY FOR four years, I drove Renee to PetSmart, where she volunteered to clean cages and feed the cats in the adoption room. On one occasion when I returned early to pick her up, I began chatting with a woman who had paused to look at the cats. Since I had become quite attached to Ralph, I seldom passed up an opportunity to brag about him and show off his best photos on my phone.

"What a handsome cat, and so photogenic," she said as she took a phone from her purse and showed me a few photos of her cat. Then she burst my bubble by adding, "There's an even better picture of him over in the cat food aisle. That's *my boy* on the bag of Blue Buffalo cat food." Her cat was a professional model.

I felt so deflated. As Renee and I were leaving PetSmart, I told her what had transpired and suggested that Ralph was becoming a *freeloader*. He needed to get a job. She smirked and said, "What Ralph really needs is an agent, and that's not you."

DURING MY CHILDHOOD, nicknames were a rite of passage for boys. At age ten, my first nickname was "Moose." It had nothing to do with the majestic animal. I was given that moniker because I owned a Moose Skowron baseball bat. When Renee was young, she never had any nicknames, but her ambivalence for them definitely changed when we got Ralph. Throughout the years, she created a steady stream of cute and affectionate nicknames for him.

Ralphie, Rufflers, Rufftalian, Ruffskin, Rufflestilskin, Ruffman, Ruff Ruffman, Baron von Ruffhausen, Lord Ruffington, Ruffino, Ragnar Ruffies, Mau, Orange Mau, Mouszer, Mouze, Mouze Man, Mouse, Mousie, Mouzington, Mousie Daze, Mozasaur, Puffle, Sparkles, Sweets, Sweeties, Sweet Tart, Sweetie Pie, Little Butternut, Tweedles, Little Love, Buddy, Curly Cat, Buddy Bean, Little Meow, Wayne Meow, and Charbineaux, plus many others that I simply can't recall.

The meaning of all these nicknames still baffles me. Renee just blurted them out as they came to mind. Her favorite was "Orange Ruffy," later shortened to "Ruffy," then affectionately modified to "Ruff" and "Ruffies." Of course, when he was being a bad boy, we reverted to "*Ralph*!"

All these nicknames were meaningless to Ralph, but he did respond to the intonation in our voices, recognizing two important words, "food" and "porch." As for Renee, she finally got her first nickname when I started calling her "Bunny." It stuck for all these years, and that is how we became a two-pet household. She had a cat, and I had a rabbit.

OUT ON THE porch one afternoon, I started laughing when I noticed Ralph looking at me from inside the house. His head was sticking out between the blinds, resembling a taxidermy deer-head mounted on someone's wall. Despite the amusement, this was a cause for concern after we read about the potential dangers of blinds and window cords causing strangulation or injuries to children and pets. This provided a perfect excuse for Renee to replace all our inexpensive, plastic window blinds. She hated them, although Ralph didn't mind. He had already perfected the technique of using his right paw to pull down a half-dozen slats and poking his head through to get a great view of the porch. He may have liked the old blinds, but Renee wanted them updated to modern cloth shades; no slats and no cords.

When the installer arrived and began the project, Ralph followed him around to all twelve windows, watching intently as he attached the holding brackets and snapped in the new shades. Ralph also found the cordless screwdriver fascinating, until the guy accidentally stepped on his tail. Although Ralph ran off yelping, he returned a minute later to continue watching the installer, not leaving his side until the job was completed.

I never understood Ralph's fearless desire to make friends with total strangers. That just validated my fear that if robbers ever did break into our house, he would gladly leave with them.

Renee and I felt sad when we saw posters in our neighborhood alerting people about an orange long-haired male cat that got lost outside on a stormy night and hadn't returned home. More disheartening, he looked remarkably like Ralph. Unfortunately, after more than a year of searching, the owner never found her beloved feline.

Always observant, Renee already knew most of the outdoor cats in our area. Whenever she encountered an unfamiliar cat outside, she would pause to investigate, checking its collar and wondering if the cat was on its own turf or perhaps had wandered too far from home. It's also not uncommon for some indoor cats to slip outside unnoticed, perhaps when a door or window is left open by accident.

Ralph was strictly an indoor cat. Yet there were occasions when he drove us to the brink of despair by vanishing *inside* the house. His disappearing act could be so unsettling that several times I considered he might have escaped, even after confirming that all our doors and windows were closed and locked. During one of our searches, I joked that we needed a tracking collar for him and a defibrillator for me. It may have sounded funny, but it wasn't far from the truth. I recall five major incidents when Ralph disappeared from what we viewed as his "life sentence in maximum security and comfort" that are forever etched in my mind.

The first episode

Ralph's routines were well-established, but one day we returned home from an errand and were surprised that he wasn't at the back door or in the window waiting to greet us. Not yet alarmed, we searched the whole house, even ringing the doorbell several times. Generally, that flushed him out, but this time it didn't.

Having traced and retraced every square foot of the house, we began again more slowly. We even checked inside a narrow, six-foot long, cardboard box that contained new cushions for the outdoor couch. The box had just been delivered earlier that day and was still lying on the living room floor. He was not inside. After about an hour, we were distraught and emotionally exhausted. Renee rang the doorbell several more times, but still no Ralph. At this point, she was standing in the living room, about to cry, when she suddenly knelt down on the floor next to that long box and peeked inside for the third time. With a huge smile of relief, she insisted that I take a look.

Wedged tightly in the very back of the box, behind six large cushions, was a pair of yellow eyes looking at us. I couldn't imagine how Ralph squeezed past those cushions into such a small, tight space. After we removed the cushions and helped him out, all he had to say for himself was "mau..."

The next occurrence

Renee was at work, and I had just returned home after enjoying breakfast with friends. A half hour later, I was convinced that someone had broken into our house and stolen Ralph. When I left earlier, I distinctly recalled seeing him in the window watching me as I drove away, but now he was gone.

I conducted a slow and methodical search. I had become quite adept at finding him in his favorite hiding places, but not this time. He had really disappeared. Before completely panicking and calling Renee at work, I launched my fourth full-house search, this time being more creative. I cut five-foot sheets of cardboard from a large appliance box and taped them between the open doorways after searching each room. That effectively blocked any escape if he attempted to double back and silently slip past me.

The bedrooms were the easiest to search. I simply closed each door after I was certain he wasn't in the room. After an hour, I was exhausted and not feeling well. I turned on the air conditioner, took a ten-minute break, and went upstairs to re-check the walk-in closet. I got down on my hands and knees, looking under all our hanging clothes and among the boxes stacked along the wall. I then had to lie flat on my stomach to look under the last possible spot, the wicker dresser in the hallway. And still no Ralph.

As I remained on the floor, thoroughly exhausted, I happened to look to my left and saw Ralph lying next to me, looking under the same dresser. He must have thought I saw something interesting. While he continued to look, I slowly regained my composure and went downstairs to enjoy a cold beverage followed by a well-deserved nap.

Act three

Lulled by a calm summer night on the front porch, Renee and I were dozing to the sound of crickets. Ralph was sandwiched between us, upside down, and asleep on his baby blanket. We would have stayed outside much longer but a sudden leg cramp caused me to jump up and start rubbing my calf. That woke everyone up. It was after midnight as we gathered up our books, reading lights, and pillows, and went inside. Heading upstairs to the bedroom, Renee asked, "Where's Ralph?"

Since I appeared to be more exhausted, Renee encouraged me to go to bed, saying that she would fetch him. Minutes later she shouted, "I can't find him anywhere. You need to come down and help me." That wasn't what I wanted to hear. We then conducted a thorough search, very slowly, because that was the only speed we had in the middle of the night. Stumbling through the house for the second time, Renee decided that maybe we left him outside on the porch, even though she had already looked twice. "I'm going out to look again," she said. With flashlight in hand, she probed every corner of the porch, and based on a hunch, she found him hiding under the wicker swivel chair, the one I assured her was already Ralph-proofed with a foam noodle zip-tied under it.

Finding him was a relief, until Renee again called for help. Our 11-pound "limpet" was not cooperating. I had to tip the heavy chair all the way back on its circular base, while Renee gently reached under and pulled him out. Twenty minutes later, Ralph was in bed, his head tucked under Renee's chin. I was not so fortunate. I lay awake for another hour listening to them: one purring, the other snoring.

Another vanishing act

Late one summer night, Ralph and Renee were in bed sharing her pillow, and we were all asleep. Suddenly, a storm rolled through, heralded by a tremendous clap of thunder that sounded as though Thor had put his hammer through the roof. Ralph sprang straight up in the air, bolted across our legs, and leapt off the bed. The storm was brief, gone in ten minutes, but Ralph did not return. Renee volunteered to bring him back to bed, except she couldn't find him. I tried to pretend I was asleep, but she encouraged me to get out of bed and help. The clock on Renee's nightstand indicated 4 a.m., before we conducted our first search with no success. After turning on all the lights, a second, more thorough search followed, but we still couldn't find him.

As I stumbled back upstairs, Renee called me to join her in the walk-in closet where she was lying on the floor. Lowering myself down next to her, she nodded for me to look at what was in front of us. Ralph had squeezed into a narrow space between two shoe boxes directly under a rack of hanging clothes. He was still scared, so we turned out the lights and went to sleep on the floor, just inches away from him. That was a calming gesture. Fifteen minutes later, he came out of his hiding spot, offering us purrs and head butts. Then we all went back to bed.

Within a half-hour, Ralph and I heard a mild clap of thunder in the distance, prompting him to immediately flee, probably back to his new cat cave. Fortunately, Renee did not stir, thanks to her earplugs. I simply smiled and went back to sleep. I wasn't going to wake her up so she could organize another search party. Two in one night was too much. With dawn only an hour away, Ralph would be fine, and Renee would be none the wiser.

Gone in 30 seconds

Renee gently woke me up, whispering, "It's time for bed." I had fallen asleep in front of the TV, and it was well past midnight. As we were heading up to the bedroom, Renee asked, "Where's Ralph?" Barely awake, I had no idea. He had been lying next to us on the couch all evening, so he had to be nearby. I continued upstairs while Renee searched for him, calling out, "Ruffy... Ruffy... Ruffy..." But still no Ralph. Just as I had feared, Renee wanted me to join the search. I tried to contemplate why a happy, content cat would want to hide from us. Are we the only pet owners who experienced this? After checking every nook and cranny three times, we started over again, going from the basement to the second floor. It was exhausting, especially so late at night.

I suggested we go to bed and let him come to us at his own leisure, but Renee insisted "we" needed to find him. The search continued room by room. Along the way, I even found several long-lost items, but still no Ralph. Renee remained on the first floor, while I went upstairs. After an unknown length of time, I heard her beckoning me to come down to the TV room where she was waiting on the couch.

"Sit down next to me," she said. "Do you see anything?"

"What am I supposed to see?"

"Look closer," she said.

I swiveled my head from left to right: chair, desk, bookcase, and TV. I didn't see anything. Renee was still grinning and said, "Just look at the TV."

Seven feet in front of me was our 50-inch flatscreen TV sitting on the TV stand with a glass-door cabinet on each end and two center shelves for the DVD player and the cable box. The TV was turned off; there was nothing to see.

"Look a little lower," she said, now laughing and pointing at the shelf where two glowing eyes resembling a periscope were staring at us from the dark recess of the center shelf. The rest of Ralph's body was submerged behind the cable box. "That is so cute," she added, and maybe it was, but I could not understand why, after all these years, he suddenly decided to squeeze into such a tight space. My next thought was that I could go back to bed, until Renee said we had another problem. Ralph did not want to come out. She tried handing him treats, along with gentle words of encouragement. He was not budging.

After I carefully slid the cable box out as far as the wires would allow, Renee had to reach inside and do an extraction. This was a hard task because Ralph had a tendency to go limp, making his removal difficult. Once he was securely in Renee's arms and the door to the TV room closed, we went directly to bed. Within minutes, the three of us were bunched together and asleep.

I was so exhausted that if Ralph had awakened me before dawn, I was prepared to go out and sleep on the porch. And this wouldn't be the first time. All I needed was a blanket and a pillow. I knew I would sleep well, or at least until Ralph's bird friends started chirping loudly before the sun had a chance to rise. This I learned from experience.

SEVENTEEN

Aloha

AFTER FIVE YEARS, the three of us were sleeping much better together, until Ralph and I made some adjustments. He started lying parallel to the head of the bed, with his head under Renee's chin and his rear paws or butt in my face. Because of my sore back, I started lying diagonally, encroaching on Renee's foot space while essentially cutting the bed in half like a fancy sandwich. This arrangement left Renee with little room. She had to curl up in a ball. From a geometric perspective, the bed spacing was split into three shapes—a right triangle, a small rectangle, and a circle. We adapted quite well until I rolled on my side and bent my legs. Ralph then moved lower and bridged his body across the top of our hips. The scene resembled a style of cubism that even Picasso would have admired.

ACCORDING TO RENEE, cats are known for sitting on reading materials to get one's attention, and Ralph was no different than any other cat in that regard. Every time I sat down at our dining room table for breakfast, Ralph would plop down on whatever I was reading. This became so annoying that I created an ingenious solution. I started reading two magazines at the same time. With my plate or cereal bowl in front of me, I placed one magazine to my left and the other to my right, allowing me to read whichever publication Ralph was not sitting on. This technique worked well until he decided to move back and forth with each turn of my head, causing a loss of concentration in the middle of two separate articles. Although I felt my idea was quite innovative, I realized I was never going to be able to eat *and* read, with Ralph nearby... unless I was away on vacation.

RENEE AND I cared deeply for Ralph. However, it was impractical to take him along on vacations, so Renee came up with a nice compromise. She ordered custom-made baggage tags with a photo of Ralph lying on top of a suitcase. Whenever we boarded or deplaned an aircraft, flight attendants and passengers would often point to the tags on our roller bags and comment, "What a sweet-looking cat. He's adorable." I took this opportunity to show a few photos of him on my phone, which always elicited heartwarming comments, except from the passengers in line behind us. Perhaps those impatient people simply didn't like cats.

ONE PLEASANT SPRING morning, Renee noticed Ralph pressing his face against the dining room window screen. He apparently was captivated by a robin's nest on our neighbor's electrical panel. From our vantage point, we clearly saw three blue eggs in the nest. Two weeks later, the newborns broke through their shells. Concerned that their nest was only six feet off the ground and exposed to the elements, I felt they could use some help. So I drove to the local bait store and bought eight containers, each holding 48 worms. Each day, Ralph enjoyed watching me scatter two containers within ten feet of the nest. The parents immediately snatched the worms and shuttled them to their hungry brood. Then a problem arose.

The extra worms stored in our refrigerator were escaping, and Renee was upset to find them wiggling on her package of cream cheese and among bags of produce. The issue was soon resolved after I put the containers in Ziploc bags and stored them on the bottom shelf. But within the week, the chirping outside got louder, and my supply of worms was gone. After I made my third trip to the bait store, the curious manager inquired, "You must be having some good luck?"

I started laughing. "These aren't for fishing. My cat and I are actually feeding them to a nest of robins."

The manager cracked a smile, replying, "I'm not surprised. You wouldn't believe how many people come in here to buy worms and grubs to feed to their pets." Then he asked, "Do you need any minnows for your cat?"

As we followed the robins' progress, Ralph continued to

observe them from his window perch, while Renee assigned each nestling a name: Steve, Pinky, and Junior. She even claimed she could tell them apart. And then one morning, we were a bit sad to see that the young fledglings had left the nest. The following spring, whenever we'd see a robin in our back yard, Renee always wondered, "Is that one of ours?"

Now that Ralph was under the care of Angie, the world's most marvelous pet sitter, Renee and I started using our frequent-flyer miles for flights to faraway destinations throughout the world. We enjoyed creating our itineraries, often venturing away from popular tourist areas to explore on our own. While these trips were personally and culturally fulfilling, there was something missing and it became more apparent as each new departure approached. Our anticipation and excitement were blunted by the sadness of having to leave Ralph behind.

Our annual trip to Honolulu in January of 2019 was a perfect example of how our feelings had changed. Shortly after New Year's Day, we made our travel lists and began our preparations. Multiple piles of clothing, sneakers, flip-flops, reading materials, toiletries, and other items were all neatly laid out in our bedroom. Everything went smoothly, until we hauled the suitcases out of storage and laid them on the bedroom floor. Ralph sensed a change. He walked directly to our largest suitcase and lay on top, listless and still, creating such a sad sight.

Two days before our trip, we left one suitcase open on the bed. Ralph sat next to it, refusing to go downstairs for dinner.

A half hour later I went back upstairs, turned on the light, and saw him lying *in* the suitcase. He knew we were preparing to leave.

The night before our departure, I turned in early. Renee stayed up past midnight, quietly sitting on the couch with Ralph and savoring their moments together. By 4 a.m., we were all awake. Ralph would now be sleeping alone for the next three weeks, so I laid several of my unwashed T-shirts on the bed. I hoped that my scent would at least provide some level of comfort during our absence.

With everything assembled on the first floor, Ralph paced anxiously between our legs until he saw the suitcases by the front door and ran to sit on them. After positioning tuna treats on the window perch, Renee carried him to the dining room where she stood holding and hugging him, while I dragged the suitcases onto the porch. When Ralph heard me open the front door, he tried to squirm out of her arms so he could join me outside, but Renee held firm.

"Taxi is here," I whispered as though we were going to a funeral. That was the prompt for Renee to set Ralph on his window perch so he could start chomping on those delicious tuna treats. It was a cruel trick we played, distracting him with snacks as we slipped out of the house. Locking the front door, I peered through the window and saw Ralph sitting far away on the dining room floor. Silent and still, he was staring at me all the way through the house. He knew we had left him. That abandoned look on his face would have melted the hardest of hearts, and I couldn't bring myself to tell Renee what I had just seen.

As we boarded our first flight and settled into our seats,

Renee and I acknowledged how fortunate we were to go to Honolulu every winter. She then leaned over and showed me photos of Ralph taken just before we left the house. He looked wide-eyed, alert, and so darn cute. Photographing him on the morning of our departure became a ritual for Renee, giving her a visual diary to ease the heartbreak of leaving him behind.

Once we settled into our hotel, it took only a matter of hours to adapt. At 7 a.m. each morning, just as the sun was rising over the ocean, we went for our daily five-mile walk around Diamond Head. Having made this trip so often, we enjoyed seeing old friends and making new acquaintances. Some of these people had their own cats or cared for strays. During our conversations, I liked to tell tales of Ralph's naughty behavior, but as the years passed, I found myself talking mostly about his cuteness, companionship, and lovability. Renee often suggested that perhaps I was going "a bit overboard" by talking so much about Ralph. She said, "I don't think these people want to see a hundred photos of Ralph." She was probably right; a dozen would have been sufficient.

Before we flew to Hawaii, friends asked us, "Why don't you take Ralph with you?" That would have been great, except that our hotel does not allow pets. And even if it did, confining Ralph to a small hotel room for three weeks, just for our satisfaction, would be inhumane. Imagine the housekeeping staff entering our room. Ralph would scamper out the door and get lost on the beach. Or what if he slipped past us onto the balcony, risking a horrifying eight-story plunge to the pavement below.

Despite wishing Ralph could be with us, we knew he would be more comfortable back home with Angie, who was visiting him every day. Besides, if Ralph ever got a taste of Hawaii—warm sand on his paws and naps under palm trees—he might never want to go back to Wisconsin.

Meanwhile, Renee and I took advantage of Hawaii's consistently warm weather. She walked 15 miles every day. I logged about half as many miles, allowing more time to read and relax. I used to think of this trip as my vacation away from Ralph, but those feelings had gradually dissipated. I now missed him very much. After only a week away from home, Renee was looking at photos of him on her phone and asking me throughout the day, "What do you think Ralph is doing now? Do you think he and Angie are having fun today? Do you think he's watching birds in his window? Do you think he's still asleep on our bed?"

Despite Ralph being on our minds so often, we enjoyed Honolulu. Lulled by the wonderful climate, twenty-one picturesque sunsets passed quickly, and it was time to go home. On the day of our departure, Renee and I sat silently in the taxi during the ride to the airport. We kept exchanging glances while smiling and mouthing the word "Ruffies," our favorite nickname for Ralph.

After we checked our bags and passed through security, we found a secluded area to wait for our flight to Minneapolis. Almost immediately, Renee started scrolling though photos of Ralph on her phone, while I was calculating how many hours it would be until our second flight touched down in Madison. Despite those wonderful weeks of walking, reading, and relaxing, we looked forward to the homecoming that awaited us. When people asked what we enjoyed most about our vacation, Renee always responded, "The best part of our trip was coming home to Ralph." I was not surprised; I felt the same.

Renee and I were still dressed in summer clothes and shivering from the cold as the taxi dropped us off in our driveway. It was quite a struggle to drag four suitcases over the snow and up the front stairs. With our bags on the porch, my cold hand turned the key to the front door, trying to be as quiet as possible. I wanted to surprise Ralph, but I never succeeded. From the window in the door, I could see a flash of orange fur as he ran excitedly through the living room and into the front hallway. As I gently pushed the door open, he poked his head around the corner to greet us.

In the joy of the moment, I selfishly left Renee outside to drag our luggage into the house while I rushed inside to pick up Ralph and give him a big hug. He immediately turned on his *motor*; a loud, continuous purr. Only then did I pass him to Renee, knowing that she was going to smother him in her arms and refuse to release him. Following our joyful reunion, we retreated to the second-floor bathroom to clean up. Exhausted from the long overnight flight, unpacking could wait. Thirty minutes later, I closed the bedroom shades and the three of us plopped into bed in the proverbial cat ball, even though it was only 10:30 a.m.

The last thing I remembered was Renee's arm around Ralph, his head snugged contently under her chin, and he was still purring. I had no idea when he stopped because we were all soon asleep until late that afternoon when the purring resumed. It was obvious that Ralph was thrilled to have us back home again, and we were equally thrilled to be home with him.

Following this trip to Hawaii, our emotional attachment to Ralph was steadily chipping away at our desire for future lengthy trips. We estimated that we traveled away from home about 50 days each year. Our trips were supposed to be fun, but leaving Ralph behind was too disheartening. This led to another epiphany: the realization that Ralph was definitely a very special cat, and I cared for him more than I did for myself. He was not just a pet. He was an integral part of our family, and he had become my dear friend.

EIGHTEEN

Love of *Nature*

KNOWING HOW SAD Renee and I were about leaving Ralph behind when we traveled, my niece Sarah offered us a solution. She and her husband Rick had purchased a webcam, allowing them to monitor their two cats from their smartphones at any time, including during their honeymoon in Hawaii.

Renee and I were excited. We researched buying a webcam and decided that we would need at least five strategically placed throughout the house. Then reality set in. We started to imagine that whenever we would leave home, whether to take a walk or go on vacation, we would probably spend a large portion of our time staring at our phones. We also started imagining our comments: "I just saw Ralph yawn. He just rolled over. He's staring at the camera. He seems hungry. He's looking out the window. He just curled up in a ball. I don't see him. Maybe he went to his litter box. Is he sleeping? Is he awake? Is he dead?"

Why bother to leave the house? We decided to scrap the idea of webcams and simply pack a photo of Ralph to keep in our hotel room.

FROM THE FIRST moment that Renee met Ralph, she recognized that he had more than just a pleasant and unique personality. He was also extremely photogenic, prompting her to take dozens of digital photos of him every day. Since she and I both enjoy photography, a competition arose to see which one of us could capture the best photos of him at any given moment. So many poses to consider: sitting, napping, sleeping, head tilting, walking, running, looking out a window, sitting on the stairs, eating kibble, or begging for a treat.

Within a month, we had taken hundreds of photos of Ralph. By the following year, his photos were prominently displayed in every room in the house. Renee also had magnets, baggage tags, return address labels, and stickers made with his image. When I created our annual holiday cards, I always included a picture of Ralph. But my challenge was trying to pick the best one, and that was a difficult task. Each year, after vacillating for weeks over which photo to choose, Renee would say, "Just pick one; they're all great." But that was not so easy. By 2018, I had accumulated over 7,000 photos of Ralph.

When friends heard about all my cat photos, they suggested I start deleting most of them and save only the best. They didn't realize that I had already deleted 12,000 photos from my iPhone. However, the real problem was that every time I deleted 200, I ended up taking 250 more. But I did find an easy solution. I simply upgraded to a new phone with a much larger storage capacity.

ONE SUMMER AFTERNOON while Ralph and I were napping on the front porch, Renee called me from work. When I described him snugged against my chest and comfortably asleep, she accused me of stealing his affections. Then the conversation digressed into which one of us Ralph liked best.

I threatened that by the time she arrived home from work, she would discover that Ralph and I had run away from home. I was going to pack four cans of tuna in a small saddlebag and strap it onto his back. Then we would hike all the way to the Mississippi River, build a raft, and float it down to New Orleans. Upon our arrival, I would change his name to Beauregard Ruffies Calhoun, and we would move into a large mansion to enjoy a life of luxury in the midst of southern hospitality.

She countered that it would take Ralph and me three days just to hike two miles from our house, noting that Ralph didn't like to walk. I countered that we would hitchhike all the way to the shores of the 'ole' Mississippi. She then threatened to seek an emergency injunction from *Cat Protective Services* to prevent us from leaving Madison. I laughed, "They will never find us."

"You will be easy to find," she insisted, "because Ralph won't make it to the end of the block, and then I'll sneak into your campsite and fly him away to Boston, where he and I will move into a wonderful brownstone penthouse on Commonwealth Avenue. He will love all that fresh New England seafood."

After 15 minutes of trying to outdo each other with our nonsensical, hypothetical fantasies about running off with Ralph, we both forgot why she called me in the first place. When Renee arrived home an hour later and found us still on the porch, she set her bags aside and cuddled up next to us on the couch. Ralph shifted his head onto her stomach, keeping his body against my chest. He obviously loved us both, which meant there would be no Huck Finn rafting trip down the river to New Orleans and no one-way flight to Boston. Ralph was content at home with both of us, and he was not going anywhere.

IT CERTAINLY DIDN'T take long for Renee to accuse me of stealing her cat again. When she began staying up until 1:00 a.m. to watch TV and read, I opted to go to bed earlier, and Ralph often followed me. Rather than sleep on Renee's pillow, he nestled on top of the blanket between my legs. I thought this was cute. Renee viewed it as thievery. Ralph had always slept next to her, and his new preference to be with me greatly disturbed her. She felt that I had stolen his affections, and that he no longer loved her as much. I told her, "That's nonsense; he loves us both."

Unfortunately, Ralph's added affection toward me didn't last long. When Renee finally came to bed, he would get up in the dark, stretch, and then abandon me to burrow his head under her chin. He still preferred to sleep next to her 99% of the time. My efforts to alter that percentage backfired when Renee caught me trying to woo him to my side of the bed with a bag of tuna treats that I had hidden under my pillow. She claimed I was cheating, but it didn't matter. After Ralph ate his tasty treats, he simply turned around and went back to her pillow.

ON THOSE OCCASIONS in the winter when Renee was away visiting her parents, I would wake up at night and feel like I was sleeping next to an eleven-pound rock. Each time I tried to roll over on my back, Ralph made a sharp-toned "mau," alerting me to be careful. Typical of any cat in cold weather, he sought extra warmth by pressing his body tightly against mine. I didn't really care because there was an equal trade-off. When my hands got cold, I slid them under his soft, furry belly to keep them warm. However, there was so much restlessness and movement throughout the night that I needed to join him for a nap the following day. Only after Renee returned home did our lives settle back to normal.

Renee's lifelong love of cats and her volunteer experience at animal shelters were instrumental in teaching me the wonders of "feline magic," a phrase she coined. However, her fascination with animals was not limited to cats. During our early days together in Boston, she invited me to view "nature" with her one evening. I took this as an invitation for a stroll through the Boston Public Garden. I was unaware that she was referring to a TV program on PBS called *Nature*. Since it was difficult to say "no," I agreed to watch and was happy I did. The episode was excellent. She later explained there were more episodes to follow and didn't have to convince me to watch. From that day forward, the PBS *Nature* series became much-anticipated viewing for us.

Over the course of time, Renee encouraged me to watch an assortment of other nature shows on television. Her love for all creatures opened up a wondrous new world for me. PBS became our favorite network, along with other cable stations such as Animal Planet and National Geographic.

One of our early favorites was the weekly series *Dr. Chris, Pet Vet*, an Australian production which was rebroadcast by CBS on Saturday mornings. The series centered on Dr. Chris Brown and his Bondi Beach clinic in Sydney. He is perhaps the most well-known veterinarian in all of Australia. With his incredible love of animals and his endearing empathy for their owners, he treated ill or injured pets suffering from a variety of health issues. He referred more serious cases to SASH: Small Animal Specialist Hospital, an excellent facility with dozens of first-rate specialists. Two of the vets featured were ER doctor Lisa Chimes and surgeon Andrew Marchevsky, who both provided wonderful care and kindness to their patients and owners.

After every episode, I wanted to quit retirement, move to Australia, and go to veterinary school, which was not feasible, considering that I had enough trouble just caring for Ralph. My time was best spent watching pets being properly cared for on TV. Fortunately, there were many other similar programs such as *Bondi Vet*; *Pet Vet Dream Team*; *Dr. Jeff: Rocky Mountain Vet*; *The Incredible Dr. Pol*; *Dr. Oakley: Yukon Vet*; and *Hope in the Wild*.

In 2016, we hit the jackpot when we watched what we believed was the finest television program ever produced about felines: the two-part series *Nature: The Story of Cats* from the PBS *Nature* series. This epic program detailed the evolutionary journey of cats from their earliest origins in the forests of Asia through their migrations across the rest of the world. They eventually branched out into at least 40 different species that we recognize today as lions, tigers, leopards, lynx, and many others, including the most popular species—domestic cats. The cinematography in this series can only be described as magnificent.

Renee and I agreed that our favorite portion of the series was the two-minute segment about the Pallas's cat, perhaps the cutest cat in the world. Averaging only seven pounds with short ears and round pupils instead of vertical slits, these compact, sturdy felines have the densest coats of any cat. They are also extremely rare, living predominantly in the rugged terrain of Mongolia and a few areas of central Asia. Sadly, their populations are declining. As for wanting one for a pet, don't bother. They live in wild, desolate areas, and the few that are in captivity in zoos are highly susceptible to infections due to a weakened immune system. However, they are indeed adorable.

Renee further expanded my horizons by introducing me to the spectacular BBC documentaries on natural history, managed and presented by Sir David Attenborough, the well-known English broadcaster, natural historian, and author. These multi-episode, award-winning programs included *Life on Earth; Life of Mammals; Africa; Planet Earth; Frozen Planet; Blue Planet; Blue Planet II; Planet Dinosaur;* and *Seven Worlds, One Planet.*

My life could not have been better: Renee and I sitting on the couch with a bowl of popcorn, Ralph lying between us, and David Attenborough looming large on the TV screen.

One Sunday evening, Renee and I were engrossed in an episode of *Nature* that featured a pride of lions in Africa. During a close-up segment that bled off both sides of the TV screen, a large adult male started roaring loudly. Before I could turn down the volume, Ralph's head popped up and scanned the room from left to right. The lion's ferocious roar was as alarming to him as a thunderstorm. Once he felt he was not in danger, he snugged tightly against Renee's side and went back to sleep with one eye partially opened. For his comfort, we turned down the volume. Minutes later, the lions started roaring again, but Ralph did not stir. He merely extended his front paws across Renee's leg as a sign of security. He knew he was safe and never again feared two-dimensional predators on the TV screen. However, he did occasionally like to watch them.

During the following summers, as Ralph and I spent idle days relaxing on the porch, I continued to search the Internet for cat minutiae, especially little-known facts that I found interesting. I never imagined that throughout the world there are 600 million cats, a total three-times greater than dogs. As for food sources, outdoor cats tend to survive on small rodents, eating an estimated 20 billion mammals every year.

They mostly prefer mice, rats, shrews, and moles, and will sometimes pursue small rabbits and squirrels.

There is currently much concern and debate about cats killing a vast number of birds each year. Hunting is their natural instinct, but because many are domesticated and routinely fed, they often don't eat their prey. Some suggest that attaching a bell on a cat's collar would cut down avian fatalities by an estimated 40%. But there are others who say bells don't work and might actually damage a cat's hearing. The controversy is ongoing.

For those who have never seen a cat's hunting prowess, just let a mouse loose in a room with a cat and watch what happens. I witnessed this firsthand when Ralph discovered one in our dining room. The result was pure pandemonium.

In today's world, with the increasing domestication of cats, a researcher in England theorized that in the coming decades house cats will lose their natural hunting traits as they become pampered, well-fed pets. One telling example came from a suburban dumpsite in New England, where a colony of feral cats kept the mouse population under control until people started feeding the cats. Within a short period of time, the cats expended less energy on hunting as they learned to expect an easy supply of food from humans. The result was that the vermin population grew rapidly. That also explains why I continued to buy more mousetraps for our house, because Ralph preferred an easy meal of tuna instead of staying up all night hunting for mice.

NINETEEN

The purr-fect patient

RALPH HAD BEEN with us for five years when, for no apparent reason, I became concerned about his health. Renee suggested there was no cause for alarm, reminding me that cats are not as fragile as I seemed to imagine. She also started teasing me when she saw me kneeling over Ralph's litter box with a ruler. I was measuring the size of his urine deposits, or "pee pucks" as we called them, and putting my findings into a spreadsheet. I had read that an early sign of kidney failure was when pucks got too large, or when cats urinated too often. Drinking too much water was another sign of trouble.

A few weeks later, Renee said I was going way overboard after she saw me measuring the consumption level in his water bowl and taking spillage into account. She insisted Ralph didn't have an issue drinking the proper amount of water. As for my concerns over Ralph's kidneys, there was never anything wrong, prompting Renee to snicker at my claim that

I would have made a great veterinarian, considering that I couldn't even remember to take my own pills.

RALPH WAS A klutz. He routinely slid off chairs and counters, tumbled into trash pails, fell into the basement laundry tub, jumped into the toilet, and slipped off window ledges. He also missed jumps onto tables, fell off the bed, banged into walls and doors, and crashed into furniture while racing on slippery hardwood floors. For his own safety, we had no dangling cords, left no drawers open, no closet doors ajar, and no glassware or vases near the edges of the counters. I once showed Renee an online ad for pet helmets for cats. She knew I was joking, but she was never quite sure. I suppose we should have been thankful that when Ralph was running full speed through the house, he wasn't able to carry a pair of scissors.

AFTER A MORNING digging in the garden, I came inside, caked in mud, and threw my dirty shirt and jeans down the clothes chute in the hallway. Standing up after removing my socks, I realized I'd left the clothes chute door open and froze with fear when I saw Ralph perched precariously on the three-inch ledge. He was peering downward and facing a possible plunge to the concrete floor below. There was simply no room in a narrow chute for a falling cat, going headfirst, to right himself.

Not wanting to startle him, I carefully reached over and grabbed him by the scruff, holding tight like a mother cat would do with her kitten. Once he was secured, I carefully set him down and closed the chute door. As I exhaled, I promised I would never again be so careless, and I certainly didn't tell Renee. However, I suggested we put a clothes basket on a table in the basement directly below the chute in order to keep our dirty clothes off the basement floor. I never mentioned that it would also create a soft landing pad for a falling cat.

Over the next week, Ralph looked up at the clothes chute door, now always closed, whenever he passed through the hallway, validating the phrase "Curiosity killed the cat." To my relief, he soon forgot this game of "Chutes with No Ladders" and returned to his favorite and safe pastime: bird watching.

By 2020, nearly 70% of American households had at least one pet, and the medical care cost for veterinarian expenses, lab work, medicines, vaccinations, advanced care, and medical supplies was estimated to be more than $68 billion per year. The average medical expenses for just one cat were approximately $1,000 for the first year, and about $650 yearly thereafter. When a feline requires advanced care such as extensive lab tests, X-rays, surgery, an MRI, or even chemotherapy, the costs tend to skyrocket. For that reason, vets are careful to explain the estimated costs to owners before proceeding further.

It's not uncommon that a significant number of people simply cannot afford these payments, especially coupled with considerations for the age of a pet or the severity of its condition. In more cases than one would expect, some owners make a difficult and emotional decision to forgo further treatment. Regardless of the costs or other circumstances, there is generally a common thread among these owners—they love their pets very much.

In Ralph's case, we paid a $90 adoption fee to the shelter, and that was just for starters. We also had to buy a $10 cardboard box to transport him home and a soft-sided carrier a few weeks later, although I had no idea why we needed it. We also had to purchase litter boxes, litter, bowls, toys, dry food, and a pooper scooper. The expenses started to add up. During his first wellness checkup, the vet explained that Ralph's liver enzymes were at unusually high levels and he needed to be treated with a ten-day course of antibiotics.

I was quite upset, thinking that we had just adopted a "damaged" cat. An hour later, I called the shelter to complain. They apologized and explained that they simply didn't have the resources to run a full spectrum of tests on every animal that passed through their facility. Renee already knew this, but I didn't. I felt it was like buying a used car with no warranty and having the engine fall out before getting it home. After I calmed down, another issue arose when we had to administer the first of his antibiotic pills. I thought it would be easy. Instead, it was a nightmare.

Renee picked him up and set him on the dining room table, while I held the pill between my thumb and forefinger. I said, "Open wide, Ralph," and of course, he didn't. His jaw was clamped shut; he was not cooperating. I tried pushing the pill through the side of his mouth, then I tried the straight approach. Renee held tighter as I tried to pry open his jaw with my left hand. His mouth was still not opening, so we took a break, regrouped, and tried again. This time, Renee had a better grip on his body, while I managed to wedge his mouth open just enough to insert the pill. After we let go of him, he spit it out.

Our next tactic involved giving him three delicious tuna treats, with the fourth one being the pill. He ate the treats, but refused the pill. On our sixth attempt, Renee wrapped her arms around him while I used *both* hands to force open his jaw, but that meant we needed a fifth hand to pop the pill into his mouth. After a half hour, all three of us were exhausted. I actually suggested using a soda straw to blow the pill into his mouth, except that the pill was too large. That probably wasn't a good idea anyway, considering that I might have accidentally inhaled and swallowed the pill myself. Instead, we decided it was time to administer tough love.

Placing him on the dining room table again, Renee gave him a bear hug, while I tipped his head toward the ceiling and pried open his jaw just enough to drop the pill in. I then held his mouth shut for a minute so he couldn't spit it out. This was exhausting, but we felt a great sense of achievement... until the next morning, when Renee found the pill tangled in the long hair under his chin. He had somehow managed to spit it out, prompting us to immediately call the vet to get liquid medication that we could inject into his mouth. This was much easier, causing less anxiety for all of us.

After sharing that episode with family and friends, I was surprised to hear about their pet experiences with vet visits, emergency care, surgeries, special diets, and pricey medications. I never contemplated how expensive pet ownership could be until Ralph had his first "incident" after only six months.

Late one Friday afternoon, we found Ralph flattened out on the middle of the dining room floor making an awful, retching noise as viscous fluid was coming out of both ends. He looked absolutely miserable. With our anxieties soaring, Renee and I looked on in horror, each hoping the other would know what to do. Being the cat expert, she suggested we monitor him closely. As we watched and waited, we looked up the address for the 24-hour urgent-care pet clinic near our house and decided Ralph needed to go right away.

Once inside the small clinic, Renee filled out the forms, handed Ralph to a staff person, and joined me in the waiting room, where we pretended to be calm and relaxed. As I looked around, I realized the atmosphere was brimming with tension and anxiety. In such a small area, it was impossible not to see and hear all the sobbing people with such sad stories. One woman's cat had eaten a considerable amount of dental floss, while another couple's dog had swallowed an unknown number of Tylenol tablets. Directly across from us, a teenager and her parents were huddled closely together, weeping on and off, while she continually apologized for running over their dog with the family car. Hearing their sadness, I almost started crying myself, except we had our own worries. The longer we were kept waiting, the more concerned we became.

I was about to stand up and ask for an update, when several staff members rushed through the room and out the front door pushing a gurney or "crash cart." Within seconds, they were wheeling a large German Shepherd past us and into what must have been their emergency room. The dog appeared motionless, and following close behind was a white-haired, elderly man. From the look of his overalls, flannel shirt, and muddy boots, he was definitely a farmer. His extremely loud crying and wailing was interspersed with pleas to the staff, "You have to save him. You just *have* to save him."

The farmer had no intention of staying in the waiting room. He barged right through the next set of doors before anyone could stop him. After that episode, an eerie silence descended on the waiting room. Everyone remained quiet, while cries of sadness and despair echoed from the depths of the building.

I changed my mind about asking for an update, figuring they had more pressing problems at the moment. The minutes ticked by very slowly. Finally, a staff person appeared, but he was not looking for us. He came out to talk with the owners of the injured dog. Everyone in the waiting room listened to the prognosis and smiled when we heard the dog would be fine. It had a broken leg that would fully heal, but the dog would need to remain overnight.

After the family dried their tears and departed, I wondered if there were HIPAA rules regarding pets. Sitting in such a small room, I had watched the whole story play out and wanted to offer my own words of encouragement, but thought otherwise. What would I even say? "Don't feel so bad about running over your dog; it happens all the time." I kept silent and redirected my thoughts back to Ralph, wondering how he was doing. Is he sick? Does he have some kind of intestinal blockage? Are his enzyme levels elevated again? Does he need another course of antibiotics? And more importantly, will he be able to go home with us tonight?

Another hour passed before they finally called for the owner of Ralph. Once we were seated in a small conference room, the first thing we noticed was that Ralph was not present. Following a quick introduction, the vet began asking us questions instead of providing us with answers. "Did you notice if your cat... ah, Ralph... did he maybe eat something soft like a piece of cloth or some material?"

Renee and I answered together, "No... no way. We never leave anything like that lying around."

He added, "Maybe something like a sock?"

I replied first, "No possible way. He has no interest in eating or chewing on socks, handkerchiefs, or cloth materials of any kind. Just food." I paused for a moment for another breath and said again, "No way."

The vet then pointed to the screen on his laptop and showed us an X-ray with a dark spot in Ralph's intestinal area. "There appears to be some kind of blockage there; we just don't know what it is." He paused to give us time to reconsider, but we had no idea what we were viewing. I was an economist, not a radiologist, but I was certain that Ralph did not eat any cloth or synthetic material.

"Well," he concluded, "I suggest we keep him overnight for observation and take another X-ray in four hours. We'll then have a staff member give you a call sometime between midnight and 2 a.m."

With our meeting concluded, we walked out the door without Ralph. Heading to the car, I felt sick to my stomach and almost threw up in the middle of the parking lot. When we arrived home, we went straight to bed, lying awake and unable to sleep. At 3 a.m., there was still no call, and now we were really worried. Thirty minutes later, I got out of bed and called the clinic. The night-shift vet apologized for not calling sooner, explaining that they had been extremely busy. He then put me on hold for a few minutes and reviewed the notes on Ralph's case.

"I see here that they took another X-ray, and everything appears to be just fine."

I thought I misunderstood, so I asked him to repeat it.

"Yes, everything is fine. No blockage," he said as he paused to read more of the notes and then added, "It appears that it may have been a clump of ingested hair that he had difficulty passing. But he is fine now."

What a relief. After the call ended, we collapsed into a deep but brief sleep. First thing in the morning, we drove back to the clinic, paid our bill, and took Ralph home. That incident would forever be known as the "$875 hairball."

Over the next few years, we took Ralph to several different vet clinics until our neighbor, Anita, suggested we take him to the University of Wisconsin Small Animal Clinic at the university's veterinary school. This is an exceptional facility with an extensive staff of primary care and specialist veterinarians, some of whom are also clinical instructors.

During Ralph's first primary care visit to the clinic, a fourth-year vet student gave him an extensive checkup, took lots of notes, and then stepped out of the room to discuss her findings with the clinical instructor. A short while later, they both returned. After the instructor examined Ralph, she discussed the student's findings along with her own observations. This was, after all, a teaching clinic attached to the vet school, and Ralph was certainly in good hands.

Renee later suggested that I may have needlessly interrupted them with too many questions, and she reminded me that I was not a vet student. She also felt I would learn more by just listening. I'm sure she was correct, but I did find all their technical discussions fascinating.

Every year when it was time for Ralph's annual wellness appointment, the process of getting him there was incredibly easy. We simply set his soft-sided carrier on our dining room floor and he calmly walked inside without any prompts or protests. Upon our arrival at the clinic, Ralph quietly stepped out of his carrier to explore the examination room, showing no hesitation or fear.

Renee assured me how fortunate we were. All her past experiences of taking cats to the vet were horrific. At the mere sight of a pet carrier, her family's cats would put up a ferocious struggle, acting as though they were about to be banished to Devil's Island. Their beloved cat, Arthur, would extend his legs outward, like an iron cross, making it almost impossible to stuff him into the carrier. Matters became even worse with their next cat, Ursula, who refused to let anyone pick her up, leading to canceled vet appointments year after year. Such stories made us realize how fortunate we were to have Ralph.

At his annual visits to the clinic, Ralph got along extremely well with all the doctors, students, and staff members. He seemed especially smitten with his primary care vet, Dr. Elizabeth Alvarez, who always greeted him affectionately, "Hello, Mr. Handsome." He was like a furry lump of putty in her hands, allowing her and the students to examine him with ease. They admired his calm, docile disposition; never any hissing or biting, and no need to bring out the leather gloves. In their opinion, he was the *purr-fect* patient.

However, Ralph felt differently when it was time for a vet tech to draw blood or administer a rabies vaccination. He didn't like needles, and I didn't like to watch. I always stepped out of the room but, even in the hallway, I could hear Ralph howling, which made me cringe. And that should have been a clear indication that I was never destined to become a vet.

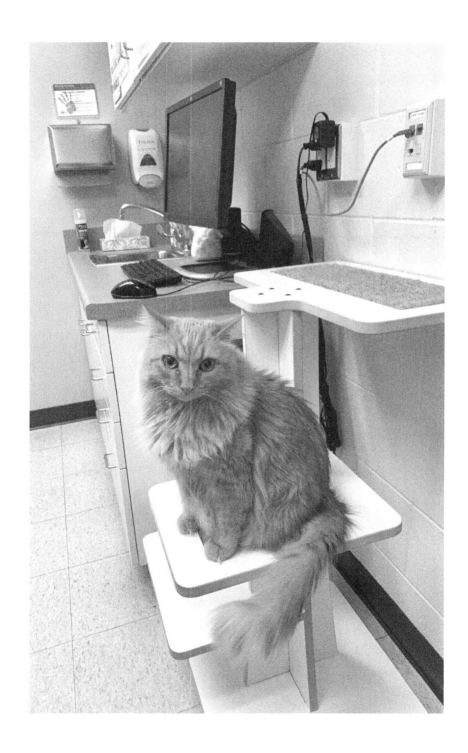

TWENTY

New Year's Day

WHILE CLEANING THE garage one afternoon, I glanced into a five-gallon bucket that was a quarter full of premium bird seed. There was also a dark ball of fur on top of the seeds. I gave it a poke with my index finger and then looked up at Ralph, who was watching me from his open window. "You would love this!"

It was a fat, gray mouse that had gorged itself on delicious seeds and had been asleep until I touched it. The bucket's smooth plastic sides made it impossible for the mouse to climb out, so I reached inside and cupped both hands around it. To me the most humane way of disposal was in a bucket of water. I had plenty of buckets, but none with water, and my hands were full. As I stood in the driveway contemplating what to do next, I looked down and saw a little head protruding out between my fingers and looking up at me with its tiny eyes and whiskery face.

"This is your lucky day, little guy," I said as I walked down the driveway and turned toward the park. Without squirming or attempting to escape, its head was still sticking out between my fingers and facing forward. It was as though we were enjoying a walk together on a warm fall day. After crossing the street, I knelt down in front of a dense row of bushes. We looked at each other one last time before I set it down and watched it bolt into the undergrowth.

"Have a good life," I said, "and please don't come back unless you want to meet Ralph."

I RECALL READING that 60% of pet owners say they often prefer to stay home with their pets rather than go out for dinner or socialize with friends. Renee and I agreed with that premise. After seven wonderful years with Ralph, we started suffering from separation anxiety every time we left the house. We even lost our desire for overnight excursions to nearby cities. Instead, we preferred day trips that allowed us the joy of returning home to a very happy cat who didn't have to spend the night alone.

By the fall of 2019, four months before our annual winter trek to Honolulu, we seriously discussed canceling the trip. Angie was a wonderful cat-sitter, but the thought of leaving Ralph again—this time for nearly four weeks—was painfully tugging at our hearts.

Renee and I had worked hard and saved earnestly throughout our careers, and we enjoyed traveling to cities across the country and exploring various cultures around the globe. But now we found ourselves reevaluating our future travel plans. In the grand scheme of things, I had never considered that a simple stray cat could one day have such a momentous impact on our lives.

On Christmas morning in 2019, Renee, Ralph, and I sat together on the floor of the TV room and opened our presents. As always, Ralph received the most gifts: a red holiday sweater, assorted toys, little stuffed mice, plus packets of tuna and salmon treats. Finally, I presented Renee with her last gift—a 16" x 24" canvas photoprint of Ralph that resembled an oil painting. We displayed this masterpiece on the fireplace mantel, the most prominent spot in our house and the first thing any visitor would notice when stepping into the living room. Ralph ignored his canvas image. He was too preoccupied playing with crumpled piles of discarded wrapping paper—*far* more intriguing than his presents!

This was a happy time for us, like a scene from Charles Dickens' *A Christmas Carol*. I envisioned myself as Bob Cratchit with my wife, Renee, and my son, "Tiny Tim" Ralph. We were a happy family, gathered together to celebrate such a joyous time of the year. And we had much to be thankful for.

Despite the happy festivities, there was still a cloud hanging over our heads. During the previous four months, Ralph had been experiencing bouts of sneezing and had a watery discharge in one eye. We suspected seasonal allergies made worse by the dry winter air. Otherwise, all of Ralph's extensive exams and tests at the clinic continued to indicate nothing was seriously wrong with him. With a sigh of relief, our anxieties over his health eased just in time.

Only nine days remained until our departure for Honolulu, but we were still overcome with sadness at having to leave Ralph behind. With each passing day, we put off the packing and continued to enjoy the winter holidays at home with him. And then it happened.

Late in the afternoon on New Year's Day in 2020, all of our past joy and happiness from so many years with Ralph were sucked out of us in an instant. Renee and I didn't want to believe what had just happened. I was in the first floor bathroom washing my hands, and Renee was just outside the door in the hallway. Ralph had wandered in to see what I was doing, and as he turned to leave, he suddenly fell over on his side. Although he recovered immediately, without our help, my heart sank to the pit of my stomach. Renee also saw him fall, but neither of us said a word. Unable to speak, we just looked at each other in disbelief.

With Renee and Ralph seated quietly in the back seat, I drove to the University of Wisconsin Veterinary Emergency Room Clinic. After we described his sudden instability, the doctor did a brief exam and suggested Ralph was exhibiting a neurological disorder. Placing him on the floor, she noticed that he was unstable and always turned in the same direction, going around slowly in tight circles. Then she noticed that his eyesight appeared to be failing in one eye.

The doctor suggested an MRI be done the following day, but cautioned us that the procedure was quite expensive.

We didn't care about the cost, only about Ralph's health and well-being. With nothing more to be accomplished that evening, the three of us returned home. Throughout the night, Renee and I kept an arm around Ralph as he lay between us in bed. Early the following morning, we returned to the clinic and dropped Ralph off for his MRI. When we arrived home, the wait to hear the results was excruciating.

Around mid-afternoon, we received a phone call that no pet owner ever wants to get. The doctors and technicians could not complete the full MRI because Ralph's vital signs had dropped dangerously low, forcing them to stop the imaging. However, the neurologist had seen enough to conclude that there were multiple tumors in his head and nasal cavity, and they were "massive." Apparently, Ralph's body was deteriorating rapidly, and he had maybe two weeks at best to live.

It was the worst day of our lives. We couldn't comprehend the reality that Ralph would be leaving us much too soon. He was only 11-1/2 years old, and we had always taken such good care of him.

Arriving at the clinic the next morning to pick him up, we received a more detailed prognosis from the doctors. There was no good news. However, Dr. Alvarez did make us smile when she explained that Ralph had been walking around in the hallways among the students, looking for affection and giving head butts. Despite his health issues, he still enjoyed being sociable.

Once Ralph was back home, he seemed to perk up, acting as usual and thereby lifting our spirits. He even jumped up on the dining room table, stepped across to his carpeted perch, and looked out the window. He seemed so happy, and

I promised him that I would never leave home again if he would only get better. Then I contacted the airline and the hotel in Hawaii and canceled our trip.

Several days later, Ralph's sitter, Angie, and her partner, Mary, walked down to visit Ralph. They wanted to give him a hug and say a final *goodbye*. As soon as they were gone, Renee and I looked at each other and burst into tears. We were completely overwhelmed with sadness.

Without knowing exactly how many days remained, we cherished every minute with Ralph. His sudden burst of energy, probably due to the steroids, didn't last long. By the following day, he reverted to sluggishness and confusion. Unable to jump up or down, he could no longer sleep with us. The couch in the TV room became his new bed, and Renee slept with him at night, snuggling together with his head under her chin.

Ralph slept well; Renee did not. She just lay awake petting him while wiping away her tears. In the morning, we traded places so Renee could get some rest. When I snuggled up with him, he stretched out on my chest and tucked his head under my chin. Each time I woke up, I hoped it was just bad dream, only to be overcome by sadness again. On one occasion, I knelt down and buried my face in his hairy underbelly as he lay on his side. He smelled so wonderful, such a unique scent that I wanted to remember forever.

At this stage, neither Renee nor I would leave the house. Every moment was just so precious. We had also taken dozens of photos, but deleted most of them. They were not how we wanted to remember Ralph, looking so weak and tired, his stamina and enthusiasm wasting away.

A final kiss prior to departing for the Rainbow Bridge.

At exactly 5 p.m. on Friday, January 17, 2020, our doorbell rang, and it was with heavy hearts that we invited Katie, a traveling veterinarian, into our living room. After a brief introduction, we awkwardly stood next to the couch, unsure of what to say next. Then Ralph walked calmly into the room to join us, in the same manner as he had always greeted every visitor. All eyes were now focused on him, still sporting his big personality.

Despite the lump in my throat, I explained all of Ralph's wonderful attributes and how he loved everyone and feared no one. He even demonstrated his friendliness to Katie, not knowing the reason for her visit. As he meandered back and forth between our legs, rubbing up against us, we explained that Ralph had been in the *365 Cats* and the *Bad Cat* calendars three times, the most recent appearance already in print for that coming March 29. I also showed her a few of our favorite photos of Ralph, and when I could think of nothing more to say, she softly asked, "Will this be a good spot?"

She then took a small blue blanket from her bag and spread it on the hardwood floor. Without further instruction, we sat down while Ralph walked between us and rubbed against our arms. He was always calm and never afraid. After Renee and I each gave Ralph more hugs, Katie administered a mild sedative to calm him down. He didn't need it; he was already at ease. In that moment, I wanted to yell out, "Stop! He's all better," despite knowing that wasn't the case.

The sedative merely knocked him off his feet onto the blanket in a deep slumber. He looked so peaceful. Renee and I took turns bending over and giving "Ruffies" more hugs and kisses. I even smelled his soft, furry belly one more time before we reluctantly nodded to Katie. She then administered the final shot and listened to his heart. Looking up at us, she said, "He's gone now."

Renee and I got up from the floor, while Katie carefully wrapped Ralph in the blanket and rose with him in her arms. She then offered him to us for a final embrace before we ushered them to the front door.

It was a beautiful, mild winter evening, and the streetlight illuminated a light snow that had been falling for the past hour. Renee and I remained in the doorway, watching Katie walk to her car. After carefully putting Ralph inside, she slowly drove away. Once her car was out of sight, Renee and I returned to the living room and embraced each other, saying, "He's gone, he's *really* gone." Then we burst into uncontrollable crying, pausing only to catch our breath. Neither of us slept that night.

Two nights later, I woke up in the midst of an atrial fibrillation episode. After taking my medication, my heart rate returned to normal an hour later. The stress levels and lack of sleep from the past few weeks had taken a serious toll.

Following a week of continuous grief and sorrow, we drove to the crematorium to retrieve Ralph's ashes. Once inside, neither of us could finish a complete sentence, but words were not necessary. An employee respectfully handed us a six-inch blue bag. Inside was a small metal container surrounded by white tissue paper. We muttered "thank you" and held our composure until we got outside. Even before we could open the car doors, we burst out crying, not caring who saw us. After a tearful ride home, Renee put the bag on the coffee table in front of the fireplace, where it still remains.

Days later, I forced myself to leave the house and drive to the grocery store where I took refuge by the frozen food aisle.

As tears streamed down my face, a woman with two young girls, about three and four years old, approached. The girls stopped to look at me, speechless, while I turned away as best I could. When their mother looked up, she sensed there was something seriously wrong and calmly guided her children away to another aisle. I remained with my hand holding onto the freezer door, pretending I was about to select something.

On my way out of the store, I bought a five-dollar lottery ticket as a distraction. Back home, as I stood at the kitchen counter scratching the ticket and wiping my eyes, I realized that I'd won $1,000. I told Renee that it was a gift from Ralph as he looked down at us from the Rainbow Bridge. This was the first time in a month that she had smiled. Without hesitation, we gave all the winnings to various animal shelters.

The weeks that followed felt like decades. Renee and I were both dealing with serious depression. Every night, we stayed up until 3 a.m. and slept well past noon. It was obvious we needed a change. Acting on impulse, I booked the last two seats on a flight to Honolulu. Considering our gloomy mood, we needed to get away for a while. Our hotel was in a quiet and secluded area, and far enough away from the throngs of happy tourists frolicking on the beaches of Waikiki. Even the warm tropical weather couldn't ease the heartache. Our happy faces masked our grief, like the unseen rip currents lurking below the ocean's turquoise waters. Each day, all we did was walk, read, and eat. We did little else. Our only joy was feeding a colony of stray cats during our five-mile morning walk.

On our last full day in Honolulu, we set out earlier than usual, hiking along Diamond Head Road, just as the sun was rising over the ocean. It was another gorgeous morning. Just beyond the lighthouse we stopped at a popular lookout point, favored for its panoramic views. Over the low stone wall was a deep gorge that ended on a sandy strip of beach far below. It was beautiful.

We stood in silence for several minutes. Then I turned and faced Renee as she removed a beautiful flower lei from around her neck and handed it me. She had purchased it the previous day, choosing one with orange flowers to which she adhered clippings of Ralph's hair. Together we tenderly held the lei, and I asked a local passerby to take our photo. After handing him my phone, he held it up and said, "Smile!"

I responded softly, "Not today."

From the despondent look on our faces, he sensed the sadness. He quickly took several photos and handed back the phone, knowing that my simple nod was a sincere "thank you."

When no one else was nearby, Renee and I faced the ocean and took turns telling Ralph how much he meant to us and how dearly we missed him. After bidding him a final farewell, we gently tossed the lei into the gorge, watching it float downward. "Goodbye, Ruffies," we said. "Goodbye. We love you."

A full range of emotions clouded this otherwise beautiful day. As we walked the remaining three miles around Diamond Head, we unconsciously dotted the pavement with teardrops. We realized that we could not escape our grief, not even 4,500 miles away in an island paradise.

By then it was already mid-March, and the Covid pandemic was spreading at a terrifying pace. Planes departing Honolulu were full, while incoming planes were almost empty. During our lengthy red-eye flight to Minneapolis, we barely slept. Fortunately, the connecting flight to Madison was 30 minutes.

Renee and I sat quietly trying console each other. We were afraid that one or both of us would have a tearful breakdown at any moment.

In the past, when our trips came to an end, there was never any sadness, only the heightened anticipation and joy of knowing who awaited us at home. When we walked through the front door, Ralph would always run to meet us. He was so full of excitement and his purrs were nonstop. However, it was not the case that day, nor ever again. Landing in Madison on that cold March morning, we endured a quiet and sad three-mile taxi ride from the airport. The moment we dragged the suitcases into our empty house, Renee started sobbing. There was no one rushing to greet us.

Months later when the buds on the trees started popping, I barely noticed. I assumed it was spring, but didn't really care. Renee felt the same. Neither of us sat outside on the front porch for the entire summer. We just read books and mindlessly watched TV. Sleeping was merely a way to get from one day to another.

With the Covid virus raging throughout the country, millions of other people had far greater problems or concerns than ours. While it was OK for me to be sad, I also had no reason to complain. However, I frequently asked myself how I managed to succumb to being so grief-stricken over a simple cat. After all, I was a guy who hated cats for most of my life. I didn't like them, and I never wanted one. And then along came Ralph, who somehow managed to leave an indelible imprint on my life and make me a better person. In the process, he had also become my best friend and, to this day, I miss him so very, very much.

TWENTY-ONE

Another year

THE PARTICULARS OF Ralph's life before we adopted him will forever be a mystery. He was estimated to be a three-year-old stray when he arrived at the Lakeland Animal Shelter. His previous whereabouts were unknown. He may have been someone's pet that escaped, or perhaps he was simply abandoned. Considering his friendly, outgoing personality, I find it hard to believe that someone hadn't adopted him before we did.

Renee had her own theory, claiming that Ralph was a gift to us from Mt. Olympus. The goddess Artemis had sent him to look after her and be her friend, while Zeus commanded him to cure me of my dislike for cats. Ralph succeeded on both counts.

AT LEAST ONCE every summer, a ladybug would somehow manage to get inside our house. Ralph always enjoyed following them around with great interest, but he never attempted to smack them down or hurt them. He simply wanted to observe.

Recently, Renee found a ladybug on our kitchen wall and named her "Betsy." Then it disappeared. Days later, Renee discovered that Betsy had relocated to the basement, where she was desperately flapping her tiny wings, trying to escape from a spiderweb. Even worse, a long-legged spider had emerged from a dark crevice and was making its way toward dinner. With inches to spare, Renee freed Betsy just in time, carrying her up the stairs and into the back yard where she watched the ladybug fly off among the flowers.

Saving what most people would view as a tiny insignificant bug was a melancholy moment for Renee. To her, this act of kindness was special. She knew that Ralph would have approved, even though he had passed away six months earlier.

Without a doubt, 2020 was the longest and saddest year of our lives. Losing Ralph in January rendered us heartbroken and despondent. During that same period, we were deeply moved by the outpouring of sympathy and support from family and friends. Ralph touched many lives, and his eagerness for engaging with everyone was widely acknowledged.

His loss was especially devastating for Renee. Years earlier, she had immediately recognized him as an exceptional cat, unlike any she had encountered throughout her life. From the moment they met, she wanted him as much as he wanted to be with her. And her fear that I would not like him was almost realized—after all, I twice nearly returned him to the shelter during his first 48 hours in our home. His mischievous behavior challenged and engaged me in so many ways. Matching wits was ultimately how we bonded, allowing Ralph's good nature to penetrate my heart and soul just as Renee had hoped.

By late spring, Renee and I found a bit of solace by immersing ourselves in gardening. We potted and planted a vast assortment of flowers: petunias, begonias, marigolds, vinca, snapdragons, impatiens, and many others. The back yard was our version of the fabled gardens of Babylon, and the greater our grief, the more we planted. It even became difficult to walk up the front steps because of the abundant colorful petunias cascading down both sides of the wrought-iron railings.

Around the same time, Renee received an email from the Dane County Humane Society notifying us that an eight-inch commemorative brick that we had ordered was recently placed on a garden walkway near the front of the building. Several photos were attached. As we read the inscription on the brick, tears filled our eyes.

IN LOVING MEMORY OF
RALPH PRESTIGIACOMO
BEST ORANGE CAT EVER
LOVE MIKE AND RENEE

As an added tribute to Ralph, Renee placed a framed photo of him on the coffee table in the living room next to his ashes. She soon added a tiny battery-powered votive light that emitted a soft, muted glow. She turned it on every Friday night, representing the day of the week that Ralph departed. I preferred to believe that the light was there so Ralph could find his way back home.

May through October had always been Ralph's favorite time of the year. His exuberance to be out on the screened front porch was a delight he cherished more than anything else. However, the summer of 2020 was unlike any other summer. We had no desire to go out on the porch. Sad reminders of Ralph were everywhere—his stack of plastic chairs, his cushioned swivel chair, and the rattan couch. Next to the screen door was his yellow gardening mat that he would lie on for hours while observing birds or watching for Ryan to deliver the mail. The mat remained there all year, in the same spot, waiting for him.

On random summer mornings when I was in the back yard tending our plants, I would instinctively look up at the window and get a lump in my throat and tears in my eyes. I expected to see Ralph watching from his window perch, his nose pressed against the screen, acknowledging me with a friendly meow. Sadly, there was no cat in the window. All I saw was a red felt Christmas stocking embroidered with the initial "R"—still hanging in his window, even though it was July.

By midsummer, after six months of grieving, Renee found solace in the company of our neighbor cat, Earl Gray. He started spending a considerable amount of time in our back yard lying down next to her as she sat idly in the shade by the garage. She found his companionship very comforting.

Nearly every morning, Earl would meander over to our back stoop and wait patiently for a much-anticipated bowl of tuna or salmon. He considered our house to be his second home, and we were happy his owners didn't mind sharing him. Earl also surprised us one day by coming up the front stairs and calmly walking onto the porch after I inadvertently left the screen door open. He sat on Ralph's chairs and took a short nap on the couch. Whether it was intentional or not, he was filling the void in our hearts that Ralph's passing had created.

Earl's daily presence throughout the summer was the perfect salve to ease Renee's pain and grief, until another tragedy struck. In late September 2020, Earl's family notified us that he had developed terminal cancer. A week later, they invited us into their home to pay our last respects to their beloved cat, "Ben"—that was Earl Gray's real name. Saying *goodbye* to Earl was difficult, especially since he had become Renee's support cat through one of the saddest periods in her life.

As time passed, I made some significant adjustments in the house. I left the TV room door open at night. I quit closing the door to our upstairs bathroom, which contains all the delicious plants. I also removed all the rolls of toilet paper and paper towels around and on top of the laser printer. I threw away the bags of dried beans protecting the wires on my desk. I even discarded the cardboard box that covered the wireless router.

I now keep the basement door open when I'm in the workshop. I leave paper, pens, and reading glasses on my desk and on the kitchen counter. I leave the front door ajar when I step outside to get the mail, and I don't close the storeroom door while fetching items from inside. Bags of cat treats and cans of tuna are still in our pantry. Cat toys are neatly stacked in a box in the dining room, and all the stuffed animals are still lined up on the window sills. Renee even sewed three felt birds and hung them over his favorite window perch facing the back yard.

We did this on purpose because we have a clear message for Ralph: everything is still here waiting for you. The cardinals and sparrows are gathering outside your windows. No area of the house is "off limits" anymore. Mess up whatever you'd like and create as much mayhem as you desire. Please feel free to wake us up at any hour, but we ask only one thing of you. Please, please come back. We miss you and love you so much. We just want you home again.

When I wake up every morning, I feel sad as I touch the empty spot between Renee and me, but I also manage a smile. As I lie in bed, I visualize Ralph frolicking happily with his new friends at the Rainbow Bridge. And one day when he sees me approaching, he'll race into my arms and we'll be reunited once again. Perhaps like the story of *Peter Pan*, this is my fantasy, and I will cherish it forever, until the day my ashes reside next to his.

Epilogue

On that dreadful afternoon in January 2020, Renee and I met with several doctors at the University of Wisconsin Veterinary clinic to get more details about Ralph's terminal diagnosis. After hearing the sad news, I recall mentioning to Dr. Alvarez that Ralph was such an amazing cat that I intended to write a story about him. To make such a bold statement may have sounded like grief was doing the talking, except that I was serious.

While Ralph was spending his last days snuggled close to us, I began drafting an outline in my head. Weeks later, I started typing notes, sentences, and paragraphs, and organizing them into files and folders. My biggest concern was to record all that I could remember as quickly and accurately as possible. I feared I would start forgetting details, until I realized that his humorous and unusual escapades were permanently etched into my memory.

I'd often sit in bed typing until 2:00 a.m., switching to a morning schedule after nine months. I also kept a notebook on my nightstand, frequently waking up to scribble notes as they came to mind. After compiling an abundance of material, I began the tedious process of stitching together the narrative. This was not work; it was *therapy*.

By the end of August, Renee and I agreed that we should begin our search for another furry companion. Then we hit the proverbial brick wall. With Covid cases soaring and millions of workers out of a job or working from home, a record number of people were adopting pets to help cope with their isolation and loneliness. Demand for dogs and cats soared, and most visits to animal shelters were "by appointment only." From August through December, we logged 1,800 miles driving to shelters throughout the southern half of Wisconsin and northern Illinois, including visits to local shelters nearer to home.

As we scoured the Internet and made dozens of phone calls, we quickly realized that using Ralph as a template for finding another cat would be hopeless. Our criteria needed to be simpler—we would look for a juvenile male, but with the condition that he had to like us and want to be with us. As our search continued, we encountered sadness and frustration.

Following a lead, we drove more than 170 miles to a small shelter, feeling certain that we would return home with a new cat, one that happened to look remarkably like Ralph. Walking into a large room where more than a dozen cats roamed freely, the one we liked approached me from behind and bit me hard in the thigh. He then walked over and attacked Renee. While the staff person tried to minimize the incident, the cat repeatedly bit her, too. We still didn't give up, but when Renee tried to pick him up, he took a savage swipe at her face and hissed his disapproval. Without making any comments, we slipped the person a cash donation and left in tears.

We eventually became so despondent that we felt *any* cat would be fine, and that was a mistake. Sadly, two had to be returned, one immediately. We struggled with the second cat, spending hundreds of dollars on vet bills and prescription medications, but to no avail. Even the shelter and our vet tried to console us, saying that we had gone far beyond what most people would have endured. The cat simply didn't like us.

During our five-month, intensive search, I amassed enough notes and stories to write an entirely separate book, but I doubt I will. However, I can summarize our quest quite simply—we finally adopted another cat. He was a one-year-old, short-haired orange male, and we named him Lou.

We were certain that he must have experienced a difficult life. A good Samaritan brought Lou to the Humane Society of Southern Wisconsin after witnessing him being tossed from a car near a popular hiking trail. Fortunately, a thoughtful staff person at the shelter had kept our name on file and alerted us to his availability. Once we adopted him and brought him home, we initially found Lou to be just as challenging as Ralph had been during his early months with us. The big difference was that I now knew a lot more about cats, and I had considerably more patience, thanks to the lessons Ralph had taught me.

We quickly realized that Lou suffered from "food anxiety." For his first meal, we gave him a full bowl of kibble and a can of salmon paté. That was a mistake. Instead of pacing himself, he gobbled it all, nonstop, in just a few minutes. A half hour later, he vomited what I would describe as a perfectly formed eight-inch, skinless *sausage*, and he still wanted more to eat. A week later, we caught him under the dining room table with a loaf of artisan bread that he had taken off the kitchen counter. That act necessitated buying a heavy wooden bread box. When he started "dumpster diving," we also had to buy a new kitchen garbage bin, one with a lid.

Lou had an appetite for *everything*, including toast, butter, jam, sandwiches, watermelon, pies, popcorn, potato chips, cookies, ice cream, cakes, green beans, tofu, cereal, pasta, bread, pastries, and lettuce—with or without dressing. Whatever we ate, he wanted his share, but we never gave him any of our food. He simply stole it from the kitchen or right off our plates. In one of his more brazen heists, Lou snatched a full slice of pizza off Renee's plate as she was watching TV. She wasn't upset, just amazed that he was able to carry off such a sizable slice without dragging it on the floor.

My solution was to buy an automatic feeder. Renee programmed it to dispense a portion of kibble six times per day. It worked well. However, during one of his allotted feedings, the machine malfunctioned and dropped four portions of kibble. Such a large amount, all tumbling out at once, sounded like a slot machine that had just hit the jackpot. Lou loved it. Within a minute, he had eaten it all and then started hanging out by the feeder, hoping for another big win. Sadly, it never happened again.

Based on Lou's love of eating, his nicknames came easily. Renee vetoed my early suggestions—T-bone, Sir Loin, and Kevin Bacon, but she loved Pork Chop, and that one stuck. Other versions soon followed: Chopper, Big Chopper, Chop

Man, P-Chop, The Chop, and Captain Hook because of his large claws. Occasionally, we also called him Billy, but for no apparent reason.

Aside from his obsession with food, Lou eventually acclimated to his new home and began bonding with us, just as we had hoped. But we often had to remind ourselves not to compare him to Ralph. They were entirely different cats, especially in intellect. If they had been humans, Ralph would have graduated *magna cum laude* from Tufts Veterinary School, followed by a Rhodes scholarship, while Lou would be forced to repeat second grade for a third time. Regardless, that in no way diminished either one's lovability.

After six months, Lou still hadn't learned to play with his toys. We bought him an assortment of learning products for pets, including a puzzle box to educate him on solving problems. With such an item, cats are expected to figure out how to open various doors on the board in order to get the tasty treats inside as their reward. After minimal thought, Lou simply picked up the whole box with his mouth and smashed it onto the floor. The cardboard doors flew open and all the treats tumbled out. That was *not* how the puzzle box was designed to be used. The ruined box ended up in the trash, and Lou got an "F" on his report card.

When we felt Lou deserved a snack, we simply tossed him a few nuggets of the dry kibble that we fed him every day. He eagerly enjoyed it. When we tried sliding the kibble past him on the hardwood floors, it became his favorite game at which he excelled. He would have made an exceptional goalie for the Tufts hockey team, possibly landing him a scholarship for which his grades alone would have excluded him.

As Lou became more comfortable with us, Renee and I noticed a distinct change in his behavior. He started sleeping in our bedroom instead of hiding in the closet, and he began sitting on our laps during the day and when we watched TV at night. He even started utilizing Ralph's favorite window perches, the ones surrounded with stuffed animals. And to our joy, he also wanted to go out on the porch, even sitting on Ralph's yellow gardening mat to watch chipmunks and birds.

While it's not fair to compare Lou to Ralph, there is one noticeable difference. In the past, whenever someone rang our doorbell, Ralph raced to the door to meet whoever came to visit. When Lou hears the doorbell, he runs upstairs and hides in the closet. But we don't care because we love Lou, and he loves us. And now that Renee and I are again living a *two-and-a-cat* lifestyle, we have mostly come to grips with the loss of our beloved Ralph. Although we have moved on to the next chapter of our lives, we will never forget him. Even now, Renee still sleeps with Ralph's baby blanket on her pillow every night.

As for me, I channeled my grief into writing this book, chronicling the epic journey of how I ended up with a cat that ultimately had such a huge impact on my life. And of course, none of this would have occurred had I not met and married my soul mate, Renee, a most incredible woman. She introduced me to the power of *feline magic*. Without her, I would never have met my best friend Ralph.

My favorite photo of Ralph

Our new family member, Lou

Acknowledgments

I am extremely grateful to my incredible wife Renee Ostrowski for her enduring patience and support. A kind, wonderful woman with a marvelous intellect, she was often called upon to read and confirm what I had written. It was not an easy task.

I also owe a debt of gratitude to Nancy Fenton, a long-time friend and a former managing editor for Pearson. She was instrumental from the beginning, advising me on content and structure, and providing guidance on the important elements of the narrative. She also did a thorough reading of the final manuscript.

My dear friend Sarah Whitney, a fervent cat lover, listened for hours and offered her support before I had written a single word. Her emails were very inspiring, and I reread them often. Jennifer Heise was another early supporter. Her heartening letters about cats were encouraging.

I want to recognize others: Nancy Howell, a friend from Boston, for her diligent copy editing. My wonderful brother John Prestigiacomo, who verified details of our childhood and his later escapades with cats. Chris Wagner, a classmate and former English teacher, who answered all my spelling and grammar questions. Angie Hickerson, an amazing pet sitter, for recollections of her time with Ralph. Walter Kopec, an artist and mentor, who insisted "give the *boy* a chance." Classmates Tom Maenner and the late Don Ballweg for their valuable help and advice; and Julie and Ryan Scheife of Mayfly Design.

Also important are those who read all or part of the manuscript and provided critical feedback. They include Sue Stravinski, Nancy and Arnie Cerny, John Sanders, Pattie Rott, Carol Heston, and Mike O'Dea. And my appreciation to Lakeland Animal Shelter, the Dane County Humane Society, and the Humane Society of Southern Wisconsin. Special thanks go to Dr. Elizabeth Alvarez, as well as the staff and students at the University of Wisconsin Small Animal Clinic... and to all our little friends waiting for us by the Rainbow Bridge.

Memories

Made in United States
North Haven, CT
08 November 2022

26417066R00178